168405

CYBERNETICS SIMPLIFIED

CYBERNETICS SIMPLIFIED

ARTHUR PORTER
MS.C., PH.D., F.I.E.E.

BARNES & NOBLE, INC.
PUBLISHERS · BOOKSELLERS · FOUNDED 1873

First Printed 1969

Q
310
P64

Copyright © 1969
ARTHUR PORTER

All rights reserved. No part of this publication may be
reproduced or transmitted in any form or by any means,
electronic or mechanical, including photocopy, recording,
or any information storage and retrieval system, without
permission in writing from the publisher.

Published in the United States, 1969
by Barnes & Noble, Inc.,
105 Fifth Avenue, N.Y. 10003

Printed in Great Britain

Foreword

This is a much needed book. It helps to build a bridge between *The Two Cultures* whose separation plagues C. P. Snow and many others. The very word "cybernetics" is a useful clue to the central meaning of the electronic revolution. The speed-up of information movement creates an environment of "information overload" that demands pattern recognition for human survival. It was natural therefore, for the first explorers of this field to use a term from navigation. In economics it has become natural to speak of the decision-making of tomorrow as taking place in a world economy. Instant access to and retrieval of information creates entirely new economic and political situations. The new information environment created by the new electric technologies is quite imperceptible and can only be discovered by special inventories of changing trends and changing human responses to the new environment.

In his new book, *The Effective Executive*, Peter Drucker devotes much of his discussion to the changing relation of the executive to time as a resource. The electric speed-up tends to reduce both distance and time so that both acquire new values. Drucker devotes special attention to the effects of the computer on management. "Critical path" programs provide advance planning of each part of a work. Each part has to be ready on time in order for the whole program to be workable. Much flexibility of on-the-spot decisions is thus sacrificed. "In its place there are high-risk decisions" (page 163). Speed-up of information necessarily entails a great increase of awareness of other operations. Nothing can be treated as merely isolated and separate any more. The total human response to any innovation becomes part of the operation that must be anticipated.

In his essay "The Impacts of Science on Public Policy", Emmanuel G. Mesthene points to the changes in banking that result from the elimination of transaction time by the introduction of computers. For example, large bank balances are no longer needed.

> "Bankers originally saw computers as faster and more efficient mechanical clerks that could improve old procedures. But, like the Sorcerer's Apprentice, they are taking over and changing the very nature of the banking business. Even the physical plant is being changed. A new bank building in Chicago has been designed around the need for powerful antennas at the skyline of the city to facilitate wireless communication.
>
> This is an important lesson to learn from our experience with science and technology in the last quarter century. To turn to science as a means is to take the first step toward changing one's ends.
>
> (page 101)

Earlier Mesthene had pointed out that science changes the groundrules of our physical environment:

> Our newfound ability to change the physical world within the same time spectrum required by social or political changes has affected our attitudes and policies in ways that enhance our use and the effects of science still further. We support much more science than ever before—an order of magnitude more than a quarter century ago.
>
> (page 98)

We would do well to consider the effect of the new satellite environment around the planet as altering our very concept of Nature. "Nature" is now content, as it were, in a man-made environment. One of the unexpected effects of the new feelings toward Nature has been the programming of invention itself. There has come a need to put invention on a systematic basis so that we can invent whatever we need to invent. But more important is the need to anticipate the effects of these inventions.

It is here that Professor Porter's discussion of homeostasis has great relevance to the social and political climate of our age. The same pattern appears in the educational sector where the trend is towards learning as discovery rather than learning as instruction.

Professor Porter's book will be of the utmost service in promoting an understanding of the need for the wedding of science and technology and of politics and the arts.

Marshall McLuhan

Preface

Cybernetics is concerned with the communication and manipulation of information and its use in controlling the behaviour of biological, physical and chemical systems. It is the basic science underlying the process of homeostasis in biological systems and automation in industry and increasingly its implications are being applied in economic and social planning. Indeed, the words cybernetics, feedback, automation and digital computer are becoming important in the vocabulary of managers, educators, trade union leaders, and in all the professions.

For probably more than 2,000,000,000 years at the time when the first signs of life, manifest in the fundamental cell, appeared on earth the process of biological evolution has moved inexorably forward. It is an extremely complex process which has involved countless interactions between biological systems and between the systems and the environment in which they have evolved. Noteworthy is the fact that the evolutionary process is predicated on the adaptation of the species to its environment and this necessitates a learning and control capability. It was the recognition that the basic mechanisms of adaptation are analogous to the mechanisms involved in automatic control systems, i.e. servomechanisms, and in many physiological processes that led to cybernetics being recognized as a universally applicable concept. Indeed, the ideas embodied in the subject are so fundamental to man and his biological and social evolution that I felt it would be worthwhile to present them in a manner that would be of interest to readers from many disciplines and to the layman. Indeed, the main challenge has been to present in a relatively unsophisticated way ideas which are having a profound influence on the transformation of man's environment.

The book is based on a series of eight lectures given to a group of enthusiastic students in Grade 13 (Sixth Form) at Forest Hill Collegiate Institute, Toronto. Evidence of their enthusiasm is manifest in the fact that many of them stayed for periods of up to two hours after school, over a period of two months. The group provided me with the sort of feedback I badly needed to ascertain the level of sophistication required. I found, for instance, that the principles of cybernetics can be understood in depth with only a minimal knowledge of the elements of the differential and integral calculus.

In the first two chapters my object is to exemplify the ubiquitous nature of feedback and to give a brief account of the historical evolution of those fields of human activity such as the development of automatic control devices and computers which subsequently emerged as the science and technology of cybernetics. It is stressed that the major objective of feedback is to decrease uncertainty and this is indeed the basic reason for measurement itself.

Chapters 3 and 4 deal respectively with instrumentation and servomechanisms. In order to control a process it is necessary to measure continuously the value of significant variables in the process. But the measurement process itself involves uncertainty and this, in turn, has a profound influence on the behaviour of systems. Servomechanisms are the generic class of automatic controllers and were first used widely during World War II in the design of anti-aircraft defence systems. Because of their comparative simplicity servomechanisms have provided models for a massive class of control systems in the fields of management, medical science and psychology—it is important to understand the operation of the simple servomechanism in order to understand the appreciably more complex cybernetic systems of life and society.

The concept of the model and its applications in science, engineering, economics, etc. is outlined in Chapter 5. The two basic classes of models, namely, physical and biological on the one hand and mathematical on the other hand, are considered together with applications. The use of models in science, engineering, management and economics has been considerably facilitated by the large-scale digital computer. This, in turn, has emphasized the importance of information flow charts which portray the schemes of dependence between key variables in a process. The model, too, emphasizes the feedback nature of many systems and model-development itself may be regarded as a feedback control process.

The sixth chapter considers the stability of dynamic systems with special emphasis on the stability of systems which embody feedback. The stabilization process is of fundamental importance throughout biology, economics and engineering, and an elementary understanding of how instability arises and how it may be dealt with are considered to be of increasing significance in the complex society in which we live.

The final chapter is devoted to the learning process and it is pointed out that trial and error learning is essentially a feedback process. Some introductory notes on the use of models and computers in the study of the learning process are introduced and a brief reference to computer-aided instruction is made. It is stressed that the process of pattern recognition is central in the learning process and that both deterministic and probabilistic patterns play a significant part in learning.

As the title implies, the book is intended as an introductory primer to a vastly proliferating field of science and engineering. If it whets the appetite of the reader and encourages him to more advanced explorations, I suggest that the books listed in the bibliography on page 151 will provide much fruitful material.

It is a special privilege to acknowledge my indebtedness to Sir Graham Sutton, F.R.S., the General Editor of this Series, whose wisdom and friendship have been a source of inspiration since 1947 when we were colleagues at the Royal Military College of Science, Shrivenham. I am grateful also to Professor Marshall McLuhan, Director of the Centre for Culture and Technology, University of Toronto, who, as a result of countless discussions, changed profoundly my ideas on many contemporary problems—not least those relating to the sociological implications of cybernetics. Professor McLuhan's Foreword to this book is gratefully acknowledged.

I doubt very much whether this book would have been written were it not for the cooperation of the Director of Education, Forest Hill Board of Education, Mr. D. M. Graham, and that of Mr. H. H. Mosey, Principal of Forest Hill Collegiate Institute. The help of Mr. L. Jempson, Head of the Physics Department, and Mr. John R. Collins, a member of the Staff of the Physics Department of the school, in arranging the lectures and recording them is also gratefully acknowledged. The extremely valuable feedback provided by the group of some twenty students who attended the lectures was invaluable and many of the ideas raised by the class have been incorporated. I would like to thank also my wife Patricia for numerous suggestions and for editing the manuscript and, most important, is my gratitude to Miss Diana Coles who typed and re-typed the manuscript in her usual inimitable way. Finally, the expeditious manner in which the English Universities Press, and particularly Mr. B. Steven, the Managing Editor, has handled the manuscript has been much appreciated.

Contents

FOREWORD	v
PREFACE	vii
1 FEEDBACK IN ACTION	1
2 MAINLY HISTORICAL	19
3 MEASUREMENT AND COMMUNICATION	33
4 SERVOMECHANISMS	55
5 MODELS	79
6 STABILITY	107
7 THE LEARNING PROCESS	126
SOME SUGGESTIONS FOR FURTHER READING	151
INDEX	153

1. Feedback in Action

"T minus 20 seconds and counting . . . 12, 11, 10 . . .". This familiar prelude to the launching of a space vehicle, with its exciting overtones, is becoming commonplace. And for most of us as the tension mounts the scientific implications of what is really happening do not enter into the picture. For instance, I wonder how many of us really understand the full significance of the countdown. It is, in fact, a manifestation of one of nature's most fundamental activities—an activity upon which all life depends. It is feedback. The term "feedback" is usually used as an abbreviation for "information feedback". Let us return to the prelude to the space shot.

The countdown process is in reality a comprehensive testing of every component, sub-assembly, assembly and system which together make up the space vehicle and the rocket system which projects it into space. It is not surprising that the countdown normally begins several days before the expected instant of lift-off. At prescribed stages in the countdown information describing the state of the rocket and space vehicle system is fed back to a control centre where it is compared with what is desired. For example, at one stage in the countdown the voltages at key points in the rocket electrical system may be transmitted back to the control centre and compared with the desired values of the voltages. If there is agreement the countdown proceeds to the next checking point in the predetermined sequence. If there is disagreement we may hear mission control announce, for example, "14 and holding". During the "holding" period engineers and technicians locate the fault in the electrical system, correct it and the check is carried out again. The whole process consists of a sequence of "question-answer" procedures in which each answer consists of a feedback of information. Indeed the sequential checking of the answers corresponds to the familiar, albeit fearful, marking process in academic examinations.

After lift-off one of the most complicated and efficient automatic information feedback systems ever devised by man goes into action. It comprises such components as powerful radar equipments located around the earth, high-capacity communication channels, large-scale digital computers (which check continuously the trajectory of the system), and inertial guidance, anti-roll and pitch stabilization systems. Furthermore, the internal environment of the space vehicle is continuously monitored resulting in the temperature, the electrical power supplies, the oxygen equipment, etc. being under constant surveillance and control. And, in addition, a continuous stream of coded data relating to the astronauts' physical and physiological condition, their reactions and behaviour are continually being transmitted to central control.

The monitoring and controlling of space missions exemplifies man's increasing utilization of automatic control devices and in many ways it represents the peak of present-day knowledge and achievement in control engineering. It is a superb example of cybernetic science. In the words of the late Norbert Wiener, the founder of cybernetics, "We have decided to call the entire field of control and communication theory, whether in the machine or in the animal, by the name cybernetics, which we form from the Greek $\chi\mu\beta\epsilon\rho\nu\eta'\tau\eta\zeta$ or 'steersman'."

Probably the most fundamental process involved in the control of a space mission is navigation. And the association between the steersman and navigation will not pass unnoticed. In starting this book I quickly decided that a good beginning might be to introduce as an example, the control of a space mission. My main reason was that the ancient art of navigation, an excellent example of information feedback, has been so tremendously important in the evolution of society. It is interesting to speculate, for example, on the profound social and economic effects of the explorations carried out by such men as the Portuguese Prince, Henry the Navigator, in the early 15th century, and Columbus and Vasco da Gama at the end of the 15th century. These voyages, especially when we bear in mind the crude, but elegant, nature of the navigation equipment, brought about the dawn of a new age.

Although the navigational techniques required in space exploration, which are concerned with navigation in the gravitational field of space, are obviously not comparable with the ancient navigational techniques, the basic principles are nevertheless the same. Guidance of a space mission, although partially pre-programmed, is predominantly inertial in character, however, such "external" techniques as celestial or star tracking, and radio command tracking, are also used. Inertial guidance involves accelerometers, memory devices and gyroscopes. In spite of the fact that I have spent thirty years of my life in the study of automatic control systems and computers I am still agreeably staggered when I read of present-day navigational feats such as missing a target on the moon by a mile or two. It will be recalled that this was achieved by Ranger IX which landed on the moon's surface only three miles off the bull's eye. And this navigational triumph, essentially a complex exercise in automatic control engineering, involved only one of the several feedback control systems embodied in a space craft. In addition, for instance, an automatic sun-sensor usually ensures that the central axis of a space craft is pointed directly at the sun, and automatically held there so that the solar cells receive maximum energy. And another information feedback system, the "earth-sensor" is responsible for keeping the radio antenna of a space craft continuously pointing at the earth.

But in spite of such spectacular achievements in the automatic control of space missions and, as we will see later, many other complex processes, it must be emphasized and reemphasized that the most complex control process known to man is man himself. Man is controlled by a vast coordinated network of neurons, nerves and muscles, which carry out his thought processes and activate his behaviour, with almost negligible power requirements, and in a manner which is far beyond our comprehension at present. As a decision-making system man is supreme. And this is the reason why astronauts sometimes take over from a space vehicle automatic control system when unexpected situations arise. Nevertheless, of course, space exploration will depend increasingly on the development of more and more sophisticated information feedback control systems carrying out pre-arranged tasks with incredible speed and precision with man acting as the over-all monitor and decision-maker.

It is perhaps worth pausing to consider the reason for introducing so many complex control systems in space vehicles and in the associated tracking and communication centres on the earth's surface. The reasons embody some of the fundamental ideas which will be considered in some detail subsequently. The first reason, of course, is to ensure the success of a mission by maximizing the reliability of the equipment. The second reason, of equal importance, is to arrange for as much information as possible concerning the mission to be assembled in order to expedite more ambitious space missions in the future. The principle of the maximum utilization of knowledge and information in life, and not least in science and engineering, is closely related to the principle of information feedback systems. It will be emphasized throughout this book.

It will already be obvious that the study of information feedback systems is not only fascinating but most important. Richard Bellman summed it up well in concluding an article on Control Theory. He wrote: "Nonetheless, for those who want to understand both modern science and modern society, there is no better place to start than Control Theory." One of the major reasons why we study the behaviour of information feedback systems so avidly is perhaps above all because they are there. And indeed information feedback systems must in a single human being, number hundreds of thousands. But in addition to biological systems we find that many modern manufacturing processes cannot be controlled manually for reasons which will emerge later, and we find also that modern economic systems may incorporate a multiplicity of information feedback channels which can give rise to unstable behaviour. As Bellman has pointed out the broad objective of control theory is to make a system operate in a more desirable way, and since information feedback is basic in all control systems the reason for our interest in it will be clear.

In order to survive, all biological systems must be in a position to anticipate the future. For example, man has built up a vast storehouse of knowledge which gives him an unrivalled ability to anticipate trends and in a sense to predict the future. Astronomers can predict the occurrence of eclipses of the sun hundreds of years ahead of their occurrence, and the behaviour of the planets can likewise be predicted with a tremendous degree of accuracy. On the other hand, the prediction of weather is by no means as accurate as the prediction of the position of planets.

A common characteristic of all systems and processes which embody information feedback is that, without feedback, the behaviour of a system would be more uncertain in the sense of being less predictable. If, for example, I try to drive an automobile when blindfolded the behaviour of the car would be most uncertain. Similarly, if the countdown before lifting-off a rocket is dispensed with the uncertainty of a perfect launch will be appreciably greater than when we proceed, step by step during the countdown, to monitor and check the performance of components. Again, when I program a digital computer to carry out a sequence of instructions I minimize uncertainty, and I thereby enhance reliability, by building into the computer program automatic checking procedures. The reader will now begin to see how information feedback tends to minimize uncertainty—this has profound significance in nature and, indeed, in every walk of life.

Man has an innate urge to minimize the uncertainty of his environment. He wants to know how?, why?—he usually finds out by carrying out experiments and he uses the results to make decisions. The decisions lead to actions and the effects of action gives rise to information feedback paths which in turn provide information concerning the success, or otherwise, of the action. And so the process continues for ever and ever.

The associated concepts of uncertainty and predictability will arise repeatedly in this book and I am conscious that these concepts, concerned as they are with the concept of randomness, are difficult to comprehend even for mature scientists and engineers. But I am unrepentant in introducing them because bright, uninhibited young minds usually have less difficulty with abstract ideas than their elders. Processes which embody information feedback channels, because of the inherent uncertainty of their behaviour, are often referred to as "stochastic processes", that is, processes which can be described only in terms of statistical laws and probability theory. Many readers will become increasingly familiar with stochastic processes as their scientific, engineering, medical, and sociological interests develop.

Before we deal with feedback in rather more specific terms, it is important to distinguish between *negative feedback* and *positive feedback*. To do this we introduce the idea of the *block diagram*. The block diagram provides a convenient diagrammatic method for describing many classes of processes and operations. For example, block diagrams are used in the early stages of writing a computer program or designing a television set or a computer. They provide us with a visual appreciation of a sequence of events and they are particularly useful in portraying information feedback systems because they show, for example, just what components are embodied in a feedback loop.

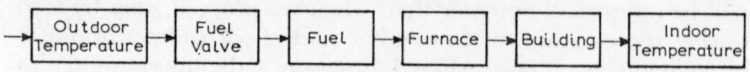

Fig. 1. Open-loop control system

One way, albeit not a satisfactory way, of controlling a central heating system would be to measure the outdoor temperature and to increase or decrease the fuel supply to the furnace accordingly. A block diagram of such a system is shown in Fig. 1. It is self-explanatory. The outdoor temperature affects the heat supply but, since the heat supply to the house does not affect the outdoor temperature, the system is an open-loop or open-sequence control. The effectiveness of a particular open-loop control system depends on how well we can maintain the calibration conditions of the system. For instance, on a windy day, the house will lose more heat than on a windless day and the temperature in the house will probably fall below the desired value. This assumes, of course, that the system was calibrated on a windless day.

The other, more desirable, approach to the problem of temperature control is to use the thermostatic system installed in most of our homes. This system is shown in block diagram form in Fig. 2. The desired value of temperature is θ_i and the actual temperature as determined by the behaviour of a temperature sensitive bimetallic strip is θ_o. If θ_o is smaller than θ_i, the furnace is turned on and if it is larger than θ_i, the furnace is turned off. The block diagram is schematic rather than pictorial in order to illustrate the nature of the closed loop and especially to show the information feedback link. The symbolic representation of a comparator unit—in the case of the thermostatic control system this is the thermostat itself—is shown separately in Fig. 3(a). Fig. 3(b) shows the symbolic representation of an "adder" unit used, for example, when a system embodies positive, as opposed to negative, feedback.

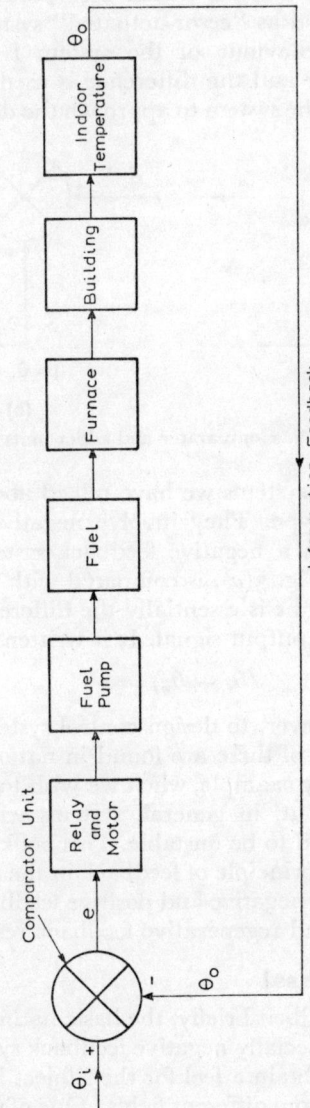

Fig. 2. Closed-loop temperature control system

All simple control systems which incorporate negative feedback can be regarded as "error-actuated" systems. This means that the desired behaviour of the system is compared with the actual behaviour and the difference is used to constrain the actual behaviour of the system to approach the desired behaviour.

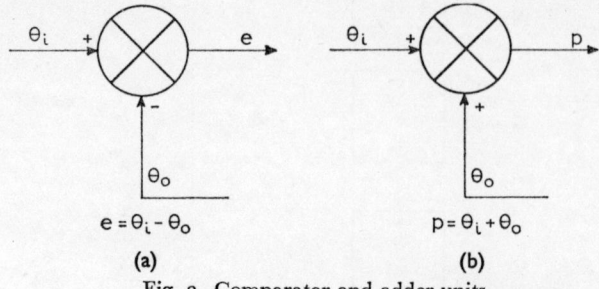

Fig. 3. Comparator and adder units

So far the control systems we have talked about have been of the error-actuated type. They involve negative as opposed to positive feedback. In a negative feedback system the feedback signal, as shown in Fig. 3(a), is compared with the input signal, and the control signal e is essentially the difference between the input signal and the output signal. It is written symbolically as:

$$(\theta_i - \theta_o) = e$$

It is possible, however, to design control systems with positive feedback, and many of these are found in nature. Positive feedback is important, for example, when we wish to reinforce a low-level input signal. But, in general, systems which incorporate positive feedback tend to be unstable. This book will deal almost exclusively with the principle of feedback in the sense of negative feedback. Sometimes negative and positive feedbacks are referred to as degenerative and regenerative feedback respectively.

Feedback is Universal

Having considered, albeit briefly, the basic nature of information feedback systems, especially negative feedback systems, it may be worthwhile now to obtain a feel for the subject by introducing a few examples taken from different fields. One of the most exciting aspects of control theory is that it is inter-disciplinary, and this means that scientists, engineers and scholars interested in a wide variety of subjects are all concerned with the feedback principle. It is noteworthy in this respect that our present knowledge of the behaviour of information feedback systems has resulted largely from the work of engineers. Recently, however, some of the most important advances in the field have been made by mathematicians. It happens rarely in modern science and technology that so massive a subject as control theory, with its immense implications in all fields of science, should evolve out of the fundamental work of engineers. A chain reaction has been triggered off which is having an impact on fields as separated as cancer research, economic theory, the control of nuclear energy, and management science.

Some of the major advances in the management of business and industry for example, have resulted from the application of elementary information feedback control ideas to industrial problems. Until recently there was little awareness on the part of industrialists that decision-making involved information feedback control processes, and that as a result these processes could be studied by methods which engineers have evolved in connection with the design of automatic control systems. This is not surprising because the whole structure of our society is characterized by closed loop situations which may be studied, for example, by computer simulation. Indeed any process in which decisions are involved can be regarded as a feedback control system, and an appreciation of this fact alone may expedite the detailed study of such systems. For example, in the management of industry, decisions are often based on the state of a particular plant or group of plants, and these states are usually described in terms of levels of activity, such as inventory level, level of wages, level of capital expenditure, level of sales, etc. The actions resulting from decisions usually change these levels of activity, and this gives rise to the closed-loop nature of business and industry. In general, such industrial systems are so complex, and involve so many interacting decision-action loops, that to study them analytically is only possible by computer simulation methods.

During the evening of November 9, 1965, a massive electrical power failure blacked-out large areas of the north-eastern United States and south-eastern Canada. It was caused by a sequence of very improbable events which resulted in the failure of key protective devices. Those who experienced the black-out will never forget it. I mention it because the problem of stabilizing a large electric power system depends necessarily on information feedback channels. It is an appropriate example to consider.

If we let p represent the "error" in the system, that is the deviation in power flow from the net scheduled power flow (in or out of an area under control), and we let f be the corresponding deviation in frequency, then the simple relationship,

$$p = af$$

must continually be satisfied, where "a" is a constant which can be preselected.

Accordingly, a change in power flow gives rise to a corresponding change in the frequency of the power supply (under normal operating conditions the average frequency change is only a fraction of one cycle per second). But if a sudden power deficiency arises, the electrical generators decelerate until either, available reserves are brought into action, or enough load is "dropped" to achieve equilibrium. If such corrective action does not take place quickly enough, the frequency may drop from the normal frequency of 60 cycles per second to perhaps 56 cycles per second, and this would endanger the generating equipment. At this stage the plants are automatically shut down completely. This is what happened on November 9, 1965.

In addition to the over-all regulation of the electrical supply grid, each individual generating station has its own automatic protective and regulating system, and its own associated control centre. At present only a few nuclear power stations are involved in the large interconnected national grids but in the future their numbers will increase. It might be worthwhile, therefore, to outline the problem of controlling a nuclear power station as another example of feedback in action. When nuclear power stations are used widely, they will give rise to many new control problems because they are by no means so flexible, and easily handled, as the conventional fossil fuel (coal or oil) fired furnaces and boilers which provide super-heated steam to drive the electrical generators of conventional stations. The nuclear reactor, the heart of the nuclear power station, will replace the conventional furnace. Instead of converting the energy stored in coal or oil into thermal energy, the nuclear reactor converts the energy stored in the nuclei of uranium atoms into thermal energy.

The first important point to stress is that the nuclear reactor is a potentially dangerous system, and special precautions are required in starting it up and in closing it down. Furthermore, the normal safety and protection requirements called for in conventional power stations must be supplemented by a complex system of instruments and communication channels which continually measure and transmit levels of radioactivity within and in the vicinity of the reactor. Suffice it to say that if potentially dangerous conditions arise (for example, if radiation monitors record abnormally high levels of radioactivity) the protection system is called into play and the power plant is shut down.

The power level at which a nuclear reactor is operating depends on the average number of thermal neutrons per unit volume (i.e. the neutron flux density) within the reactor core.

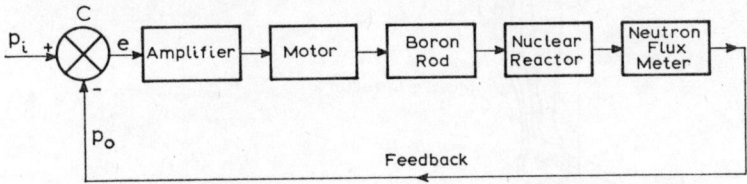

Fig. 4. Block diagram of nuclear reactor control system

If the neutron flux density is too high, the operating temperature of the reactor is usually too high and may affect adversely the operation of the steam turbines. To control the level of activity of the reactor a series of so-called control and shut-down rods, usually boron rods, are inserted to varying depths within the reactor core. Boron has the property of absorbing thermal neutrons and thereby preventing them from producing nuclear fission which in turn creates more thermal neutrons, and so on. It will be recalled that nuclear fission is the process whereby a thermal neutron in the close vicinity of a nucleus of uranium 235 may cause the nucleus to split into the nuclei of two lighter elements and in so doing to release energy. The regulation of the power level of operation of the nuclear reactor is achieved by controlling the position of the boron rods according to a scheme shown in block diagram form in Fig. 4.

We assume that the neutron flux density within the reactor can be measured and that we have the capability of controlling the rod positions by means of electric motors. Having decided on the desired power level of operation of the reactor, this value is set on a dial and the setting corresponds to p_i in the diagram. The actual power level of operation, p_o, is measured by the neutron flux density meters, and the information is fed back and compared with the desired value as shown. If, for example, the actual power level is lower than the desired level, the error signal e, obtained as an electrical signal from the comparator (C), is amplified by a conventional electronic amplifier,

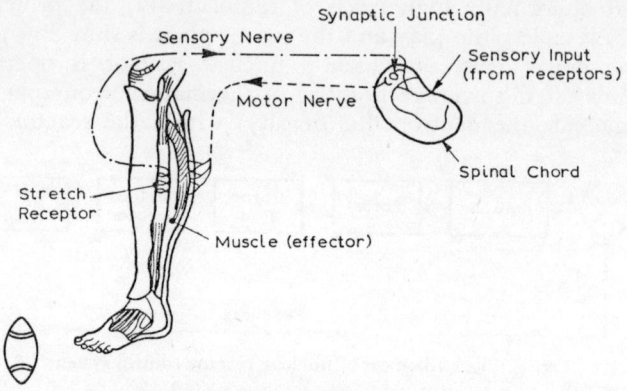

Fig. 5. Physiological feedback system

and the signal is then applied to the terminals of electric motors which rotate in such a direction as to lift, or pull, the boron control rods out of the reactor core. This process continues until the actual operating power level is the same as the desired operating power level. Alternatively, if the actual power level is greater than the desired power level, the error signal e has the opposite sign to that in the previous situation, and the amplified signal causes the motors to rotate in such a direction as to insert the control rods further into the reactor core. The closed cycle nature of the control operation will be obvious and it is still more obvious when we see it portrayed in Fig. 4.

We turn now to a biological information feedback control system. In total there are probably many millions of information feedback processes in the human body. The complexity of most biological control systems is still beyond the understanding of neuro-physiologists although considerable progress is being made.

Consider, for example, a very simplified neural feedback system. Suppose I have decided to kick a football. The decision is originally made in a small part of the cerebral cortex of my brain and a message is transmitted via the spinal cord to a particular set of nerve cells in the spinal cord which are connected to the muscles of my leg and foot. One of these nerve cells with its output motor fibre and its input sensory fibre is shown schematically in Fig. 5. The single sensory input signal from the brain controls the single motor output. A feedback signal, actuated by the so-called stretch receptor, sends a signal back to the nerve cell to confirm that the command has in fact been carried out.

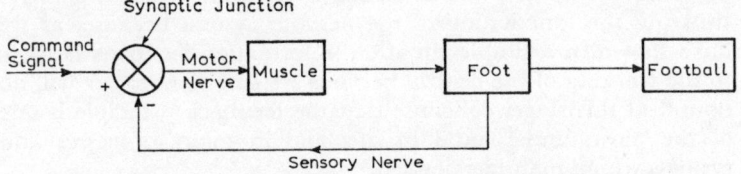

Fig. 6. Block diagram of physiological feedback system

The synaptic junction shown in the diagram acts as the control comparator unit (or local decision-making element) and switches off the nerve cell activity when the desired action, in this case kicking a football, has been completed. Of course, this is a very elementary explanation of an extremely complex process but it at least demonstrates the importance of information feedback in our bodies. The equivalent block diagram is shown in a simplified form in Fig. 6.

An elementary introduction to the feedback principle would not be complete without mention of the idea of homeostasis. The human body, in a normal healthy state, may be regarded as being in a state of equilibrium with respect to many key variables. For example, the temperature of the body remains approximately constant regardless of large changes in outside temperature, perhaps from −40°F to 100°F, assuming, of course, suitable clothing is worn. Another homeostatic mechanism is that which ensures an adequate supply of oxygen to the cells of the body.

Another system controls the diameter of the pupil of the eye so that the retina of the eye is not damaged by too intense light, on the one hand, and on the other hand, in conditions of poor illumination, the pupil is sufficiently wide open to ensure as much light as possible reaching the retina. Other mechanisms which are usually regarded as homeostatic are responsible for maintaining constant levels of sugar, protein, sodium, calcium, etc. in the blood and others induce the clotting of blood in cases of injury. This fantastically complex biological control system is predicated on countless information feedback channels which in total comprise the so-called autonomic nervous system. This system, which provides a paradise for the cyberneticist, is concerned with the control of the internal environment of the body so that it can cope with its external environment. Cybernetics, the study of control in all forms, is naturally concerned with studying the functioning of the nervous system because, as we have shown in a simple situation, information feedback is basic to the working of the central nervous system. The reader will no doubt, at this stage, conclude that the feedback principle is one of the most fundamental in life, and in many processes and systems which man has devised.

Before concluding our brief glimpse at feedback in action, it may not be out of place to refer to the significance of information feedback in a nation's economy. Unfortunately, as in the cases of biological control systems, economic regulatory processes, because they involve large numbers of people, and because people are on the whole unpredictable, are very complex. Paradoxically, even the high precision navigational control systems of space vehicles and the control systems of nuclear power stations are comparatively very simple.

Suppose a government decides that the economy of a country will be healthy if a desired rate of spending, say S_d dollars, or pounds, etc. per month, is maintained. If, however, the actual level of rate of spending is S_a dollars per month, and this is higher than the desired level, we say a state of inflation or an inflationary tendency exists. To deal with this the government may request the banks to raise the interest level on bank loans in order to correct the tendency towards inflation. On the other hand, if the actual level of spending is below that desired, it would be necessary to stimulate the economy by reducing the interest rate.

The process of adjusting the interest rate, in accordance with the level of activity of the economy, is an example of a negative feedback control system. A simple block diagram which gives a pictorial description of the system is shown in Fig. 7. Its negative feedback characteristic is shown clearly. A simple mathematical description of the system is outlined below:

Let S_d = desired level of spending,
S_a = actual level of spending,

Then e = difference = $S_d - S_a$

Assume R = interest level = $(R_o + r)$, in which R_o = standard level of interest, and $r = -ke$ is the change in interest, dependent upon e, which provides the control.

The simplified equations of the economic system can now be written,

$$S_d - S_a = e$$
$$R = R_o - ke$$

and Fig. 7 is the corresponding block diagram representation.

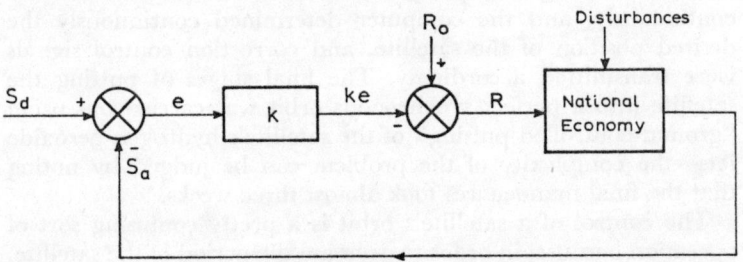

Fig. 7. A simple economic control system

As a last example in this brief survey of systems and processes which are characterized by information feedback we will consider one of the multitude of feedback control problems of space technology. I refer to the control of so-called synchronous satellites. They are potentially of great importance in world communications, and already provide us with the means of transmitting some television programmes between continents.

The well-known law of planetary motion, Kepler's third law, which states that "the square of the periods of revolution of different planets stand in the same ratio as the cubes of their mean distances from the sun", provides the basis for the principle of the synchronous satellite. If, for example, a satellite is put into a circular equatorial orbit at an altitude of 22,237 miles above the surface of the earth, its period of revolution will be the same as the earth's period of rotation. Observed from the earth the satellite appears to be stationary, and hence its potential value in the transmission of radio and television signals continuously between continents. But the task of putting a satellite into a synchronous orbit is complex, and from our present point of view it represents an exceptionally elegant application of information feedback control. For example, SYNCOM III which was launched into orbit in August, 1964, was manoeuvred into a nearly synchronous equatorial orbit by a sequence of moves under the control of an earth tracking and control station. These manoeuvres took a total of 29 hours after lift-off and for the most part were determined by "on-line" (that is, working in true time) computer calculations. In this particular information feedback control system information, defining the position of the satellite, was received continuously, and the computer determined continuously the desired position of the satellite, and correction control signals were transmitted accordingly. The final stages of putting the satellite into a perfect synchronous orbit was carried out using "ground-controlled pulsing" of the satellite's hydrogen-peroxide jets—the complexity of the problem can be judged by noting that the final manoeuvres took almost three weeks.

The control of a satellite's orbit is a pretty confusing sort of operation because, in order to decrease the period of the satellite, and hence to increase its steady-state linear speed relative to the earth's surface, it must initially be slowed down by firing retroactive rockets—no wonder a computer is needed to determine what the next move must be!

A Hierarchy of Control Systems

It is convenient to consider a hierarchy of information feedback control systems based on the amount of information which is actually fed back. As we have seen most processes, whether chemical, mechanical, electronic, biological, or economic, must be controlled and hence must embody information feedback.

But in some cases it is only necessary to incorporate feedback channels in order to provide protection. From the point of view of the amount of data fed back a protection system is a first-level control. For example, in the nuclear reactor control system, considered previously, the protection circuits, although continually monitoring the state of the system, become closed loop systems only when danger threatens and the protection system causes a partial or complete shutdown of the reactor. Another example of a protective system is the fire protection system which goes into action only when a fire is located—in this case feedback signals, perhaps from a public fire-call box, or an automatic fire alarm, feed signals back to the Fire Brigade Control Room and corrective action is taken immediately. Protection systems, although at the lowest level of our hierarchy of information feedback control systems, are nevertheless vitally important. Life could not exist without them.

The second level of control includes automatic regulator systems such as, for example, the thermostatic control of the temperature of our homes. Automatic regulators are widespread in nature and in our man-made environment. In the manufacture of chemical products, for example, many regulatory processes involving the control of temperature, pressure, flow, liquid level, etc. are frequently involved.

In automatic regulators we measure continuously, or sample at regular intervals, the value of a control variable (say a temperature) and compare it with a pre-set desired value. The control of the process is actuated by the difference between these values. As I pointed out previously the system can be regarded as "error-actuated". This class of system has been subjected to intensive study and experimentation by scientists and engineers, and the design of single-loop regulating systems has reached a high level of precision. Witness the three miles off bull's eye moon shot.

The next higher level in the hierarchy of feedback control systems can be described as optimal control systems. In these it is not only necessary to regulate the values of selected control variables in accordance with their desired values, but we must ascertain continually what the desired values should be to satisfy pre-determined goals. For example, in a space mission to the moon several important requirements must be satisfied.

One of them is the optimum utilization of fuel. In other words the trajectory from earth to moon must be an optimum trajectory in order to minimize fuel requirements. Similarly, in a chemical process it is usually desired to maximize the yield of the process and, because of continually changing conditions, this means determining continually the most appropriate desired values of the control variables in order to meet the maximum yield requirement. Optimal control systems of this kind frequently require the processing of large amounts of data and this is only practicable through the use of high-speed computers. I should perhaps point out that optimal control systems are a comparatively recent development in the field of control theory—such systems were almost unheard of a mere ten years ago.

At the top of the hierarchy of control systems are the multivariable automatic adaptive control systems which at present we are incapable of designing. But most biological systems, and certainly the human body, incorporate large numbers and a remarkable variety of such highly complex adaptive systems. The object of an adaptive control system is to change its internal structure or circuitry in order to optimize its behaviour in spite of continuous changes in the environment. The human brain is by far the most complex adaptive controller known to man. It changes its internal organization every second or two in order to deal with new problems and new situations. Unfortunately I can say very little about adaptive control systems except perhaps that they normally embody a multiplicity of feedback paths, they embody pattern recognition capabilities and the means for storing these patterns, and they embody search mechanisms which continuously probe the environment in order to update their internal structure and the patterns which have been built up. But on account of the complex interactions between the controlled variables, and the uncontrolled variables of the environment, the problem of analysing and synthesizing such systems is at present far beyond our capabilities.

In this book we will consider, for the most part, automatic regulators of various kinds because on account of their comparative simplicity they best exemplify the principle of feedback.

2. Mainly Historical

The history of information feedback systems, and for that matter the whole evolution of automation, embraces pretty well the complete history of technology. It would be most unwise to try even to summarize how this vast subject has developed. On the other hand, as in all fields of science and technology, a glimpse into the past, however brief, is usually essential in order to put things into perspective. Indeed, the task of organizing and structuring knowledge depends essentially on the assembling of appropriate information, and data, and this is what history can provide.

Man's ability to communicate and to store knowledge is one of the important characteristics which sets him apart from the other animals. And it is therefore important that we should make full use of what we can glean from the past. This is the justification for introducing a brief history of cybernetics.

Perhaps a suitable starting point is to mention that the process of evolution, or natural selection, itself relies heavily on the pattern recognition capabilities of a species. That is, the ability of a member of the species, say a man, to recognize a potentially dangerous situation on the one hand, or perhaps a potentially desirable trend on the other. This recognition process inevitably requires information feedback because it involves comparisons with past experience. The associated decision-making, and action processes, will be based on whether or not a situation confronting us is likely to be benign or unpleasant. Another way of looking at it is that most biological systems are necessarily goal-seeking, and by its very nature goal-seeking involves negative feedback.

Cybernetics, the science of control and communication in man and machine, is generally assumed to be a recently invented subject. Indeed, as I mentioned in the last chapter, the term cybernetics was coined by the late Professor Norbert Wiener only twenty years ago. But the subject had roots which were established many centuries ago.

During World War II, extensive research in the theory and practice of anti-aircraft gunnery, and more especially the problem of predicting the position of aircraft targets perhaps a minute ahead of their present position, was carried out and a mathematical theory of prediction was developed. And, as we have already seen, since accurate prediction reduces uncertainty this research turned out to be one of the most important contributions to the science of control. But Wiener carried the subject much further when he pointed out the analogous behaviour demonstrated by some automatic control systems and computers, on the one hand, and the behaviour of some biological processes on the other. He was particularly impressed with the parallels which exist, for example, between sequences of high-speed switches in computers and sequences of neurons in the central nervous system. Both have "on-off" characteristics. The sort of question which Wiener and his colleagues were asking at the time (1946) was, "What is the mechanism by which we recognize a square as a square, irrespective of its position, its size, and its orientation?" Such questions are still being asked today. We know, of course, that the feedback principle is involved but how the memory and the associated sensory nerve fibres are organized in the recognition process is still a mystery. But we are well ahead of the story and it is now necessary to delve farther back into history.

In the prehistoric age when man first became identified as "homo sapiens" his adaptation to a very hostile environment probably gave rise to the enhancement of the coordination of his hand, eye and ear. And this in turn, during tens of thousands of years, perhaps gave rise to man's massive brain. Man's ability to communicate with his fellows and to fashion crude tools to expedite his hunting were also characteristic of this age.

There is evidence that astronomy and subsequently navigation were perhaps man's earliest scientific pursuits. It is noteworthy, also, that the science of navigation is in the forefront of problems in modern space technology and it will unquestionably lead to important advances in astronomy. And, of course, the very word cybernetics puts the spotlight on navigation and hence on the feedback principle.

The Greeks, especially Hipparchus, whose work in astronomy probably ranks far above that of any other astronomer of the

Ancient World, were the world's first great astronomers. Hipparchus, for instance, was the inventor of trigonometry and, by his meticulous and patient measurements, using the crudest of instruments, he classified over one thousand stars according to brightness. His list of constellations has undergone few alterations to the present day. Hipparchus also originated the idea of specifying a point on the earth's surface by longitude and latitude. He was perhaps the founder of empirical science and, because of his emphasis on precision measurement, his celestial charts provided the early navigators with the means for laying and keeping a course. I regard Hipparchus as perhaps the first cyberneticist.

The term navigation can, of course, be used in a wide variety of ways. For example, we can think of ourselves as being navigated through "educational space". We set ourselves goals and our teachers, libraries and laboratories help us navigate towards these goals. If we depart from the prescribed path, some corrective action is needed—we are, in fact, applying the principle of feedback. Similarly, when we navigate our cars and bodies through physical space we involve at all times the feedback principle.

We must bear in mind when we are discussing the feedback principle and, in particular, when we are examining the historical background, that one of the most important modern applications of the feedback principle is to automation. And automation in its broadest sense began when Paleolithic man fashioned crude stone tools to help him in his continual hunt for food. Man has always been a tool-maker and we have come to regard his tools, however complex, like computers, to be extensions of himself.

Although the first crude implements of early man scarcely justify being described as tools, they nevertheless constitute the main trunk of what we can regard as the evolutionary tree of mechanization and automation. However, the tools of the Stone Age and the appreciably more sophisticated tools, instruments and weapons of the Bronze, Copper, and Iron Ages, which followed, did not involve automatic operation. But the use of hand tools, necessitating the coordination of eye and hand, was based essentially on the feedback principle, as indeed most conscious actions are. And it is important to note that at an early stage in our history the use of hand tools gave rise to the fashioning of fairly elaborate human and animal-powered machines.

Frequently, especially in modern times, scientists and engineers are considered to be materialistically-oriented people, perhaps even lacking in culture. But it must be stressed, over and over again, that throughout his evolution man has had an innate urge to simulate himself and the world about him irrespective of whether or not material good has resulted. Thus the early tools and mechanical artifacts which man contrived were not merely for the purposes of hunting, or agriculture, or domestic chores in general, but just as important they satisfied a deep-seated urge to create. The extraordinary influence which man's urge to simulate himself has had on the cultural history of mankind cannot be overemphasized.

Examples of man the creator are of course widespread throughout history. We find them in the form of the dolls with jointed arms discovered in Ancient Egyptian tombs, and in the mechanical objects produced in Greek and Roman times which have been revealed as ingenious devices used, not as machines, but essentially as rather trivial toys. And perhaps the supreme modern example of man striving to simulate his own behaviour is manifest in the digital computer. This is interesting speculation which may have a more profound impact on our cultural evolution than it is sometimes credited with.

An important chapter in the history of cybernetics was written during the 14th, 15th and 16th centuries when some of the early automata were developed. These frequently took the form, as mentioned previously, of models of men and animals operated by the hour striking mechanisms of large clocks. Many such automata have survived in working condition until the present day. Some historians of science and technology have traced the link between these earlier automata and modern automation systems. There is no doubt that the many basic inventions incorporated in the automata led to significant developments in industrial machinery, which subsequently gave rise to the industrial machines which blossomed during the Industrial Revolution (18th and early 19th centuries). Indeed, it is not untrue to say, for example, that cybernetics, as we understand the term today, was already at a stage of potential realization some two hundred years ago.

Although James Watt, who, in 1788, invented the steam engine fly-ball governor, which is still in widespread use today, is often credited as being the first man to design a feedback control system, I believe there is adequate evidence to show that several inventors and scientists consciously contrived automatic feedback control systems at least a hundred years before Watt. One such inventor was Cornelius Drebbel (1573–1633), a Dutchman. He designed a thermostatically controlled furnace and incubator which he used for rearing chickens. And, about 1680, a Frenchman, Denis Papin, introduced the idea of automatic pressure regulation. By putting a weight on the lid of a domestic cooking pan, and thereby ensuring that the lid lifted when steam pressure inside the pan reached a given level, he anticipated the steam safety valve (and incidentally, of course, the pressure cooker), and this is one of the most widely used of all automatic regulators. Although the feedback link in this system is not obvious it will be clear that the principle of operation is predicated on the comparison of an actual with a desired behaviour.

During the 18th century we find the increasing utilization in industry of wind power and steam power. And the need to control these sources of power led to two extremely important inventions in the field of automatic regulation. The first related to the control of windmills; it was the "fantail", used to turn the sails into the wind, together with a feathering mechanism, which adjusted the inclination of "shutters" on the sails, and automatic control of speed was achieved.

The second important invention was the "centrifugal governor", designed by James Watt, to control the speed of his steam engine. The principle of the Watt speed governor is illustrated in Fig. 8. In normal operation the governor is adjusted so that linkage AB is level. If, however, the load on the steam turbine decreases the speed of the turbine shaft X will increase and this will cause the balls of the governor P and Q to increase their radius of rotation (due to the centrifugal force acting on them) so that the governor collar B rises and, through the lever action, the steam valve V closes or partially closes. On the other hand if the load driven by the steam turbine increases the turbine shaft velocity will decrease, the radius of rotation of the governor balls will decrease, the collar B will descend and the steam valve will be open. In the case of the speed governor the feedback link comprises the lever *AB*, the amplifier, and the rod *R* controlling the opening or closing of the steam valve. The desired speed setting of the system is controlled by the positioning of the linkage *AB* and the sensitivity of the system will depend upon such factors as the weight of the fly-balls, the stiffness and setting of the constraining spring and the positioning of the pivot *F*.

The theory of the Watt speed governor was first worked out by Clerk Maxwell in 1868—Norbert Wiener has referred to this. He writes, "We wish to recognize that the first significant paper on feedback mechanisms is an article on governors, which was published by Clerk Maxwell in 1868."

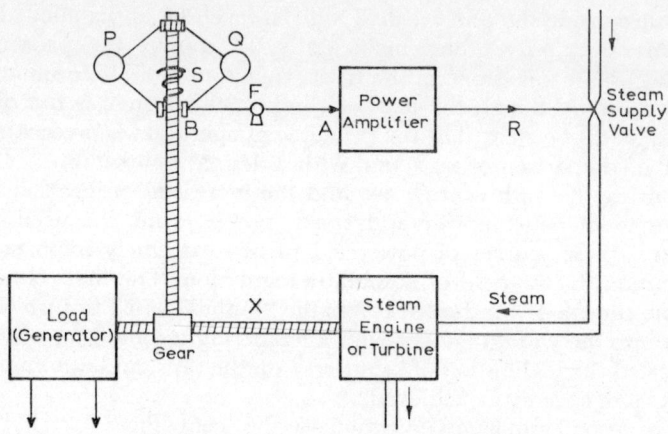

Fig. 8. Principle of fly-ball speed governor

We must note also that, following in the tradition which gives navigation science an honoured place in the evolution of feedback control systems, the steering engines of ships were some of the earliest and best developed forms of automatic feedback controls. It was a Frenchman, Farcot, who, in 1872, introduced the first servo-assisted ship steering engine. With the advent of larger and heavier ships the need for power-assisted rudder positioning mechanisms was acute at that time. Today, of course, we have servo-steering in automobiles. And in jet airliners a vast multiplicity of servomechanisms, actuated by the pilot, control the positioning of the control surfaces which determine the direction of flight. Manual operation, with no power assistance, of systems such as aircraft rudder and aileron controls would clearly be physically impossible.

I am not aware of any other major new development during the 19th century in which the feedback principle was applied or studied. But early in the present century, especially during World War I, the field became of increasing importance because of its significance in naval gunnery. The positioning of massive naval gun turrets weighing hundreds of tons was not a job for man, not even for a team of hefty seamen! The hydraulic servomechanisms which were developed in time for World War II were models of mechanical excellence and precision and have provided modern industry with a wide variety of hydraulic amplifiers and motors.

It is not possible, however, to give even a brief summary of the spectacular innovations in automatic feedback control system design which have been introduced during the present century. But it is worthwhile to single out a few of the key

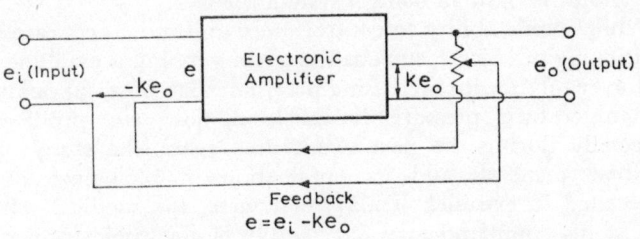

Fig. 9. Electronic negative feedback amplifier

inventions, and discoveries, which have played a notable part in the development of modern control science and engineering.

The invention, in 1931, of the negative feedback electronic amplifier by Nyquist and Black of the Bell Telephone Laboratories, and the subsequent theory of these systems leading to the now famous Nyquist criterion of stability (1932), must surely rank as cornerstones in the evolution of feedback control technology. It is not coincidental that these developments were first used in the design of radio receivers. The principle of the negative feedback amplifier is illustrated in Fig. 9. The object of this special amplifier is to ensure that the shape of the output signal follows closely the shape of the input signal. And since a fundamental requirement of all radio, and television, channels is to reproduce a transmitted signal with minimum distortion, the significance of the negative feedback amplifier in radio communication will be apparent.

If the amplification factor is made very large then the difference between input signal e_i and output signal e_o will be very small. Ideally, by increasing the "gain" of the amplifier the "error" in the feedback amplifier can be made infinitesimally small. For example, if the amplifier has a gain of one million, an error signal of one ten-thousandth of a volt still produces an amplifier output of one hundred volts. But unfortunately, and this is very significant, a point is reached, as we use increasing values of gain, when the system begins to oscillate uncontrollably. This is characteristic of most information feedback systems in which a power amplifier is involved. The study of the oscillatory behaviour of such systems, and how to minimize oscillatory behaviour, is basic in control system theory.

While man's ability to control more and more accurately the positioning of objects, such as the cutting tool of a machine tool, and to regulate with increasing precision such physical quantities as temperature, pressure, liquid level, flow, etc. proliferated, especially during the past twenty-five years, the study of the feedback principle and its application in biological systems proceeded in parallel. Today, of course, the medical scientist has at his command a large assembly of electronic instrumentation and information feedback systems for the study of complex phenomena. But in the 1920's, when W. B. Cannon and his colleagues at Harvard began studies of information feedback systems in the human body, there was minimal collaboration between medical scientists and engineers. Cannon, for example, introduced the term "homeostasis" in referring to the condition of "physiological equilibrium" which is characteristic of all forms of life. The fact that homeostasis is a process in which a large number of information feedback systems are involved is clearly evident in Cannon's book "The Wisdom of the Body". The temperature regulation of the body, the regulation of the sugar content of the blood, the coagulation of blood and blood clotting in the case of injuries involving loss of blood, are all manifestations of the feedback principle operating in such a way as to keep our bodies in a state of optimum efficiency.

It is sometimes not appreciated that research workers in fields other than physics and engineering frequently make important contributions to advances in these fields. Cannon's work, for instance, constituted an important landmark in the evolution of cybernetics.

We have already emphasized the universal applicability of the feedback principle. But information feedback would clearly be impossible unless means for transmitting information from one point to another were available. We describe the operation of transferring information between two points as that of communication. And communication, whether by speech, or books, or radio, or newspapers and magazines, etc. is man's most powerful attribute. I introduce it at the present juncture because so much of modern feedback control theory has been based on communication theory. This has been most apparent during the past thirty years. And, not surprisingly, our ability to transmit large amounts of information at high speed over long and short distances has, on the one hand, given rise to such spectacular developments as the control of space vehicles which may be many millions of miles away, and the development of high-speed digital computers, involving ultra-high speed transfers of information between major units, on the other. We will consider briefly two developments in communication science and engineering which have had, and are having, a profound influence on the development of control systems. I refer to the invention of radar and to the development of special coding systems which are required in many information channels.

With the advent of radar, and its use during World War II in naval and anti-aircraft gunnery, it soon became obvious that manual operation of the equipment was inadequate to cope with the problem of tracking high-angular acceleration and rate aircraft targets. It was necessary to eliminate the human operators and to design automatic tracking equipment which "locked" a radar antenna on to an aircraft target. This problem called for a high degree of engineering skill especially in the field of electronics. It was solved originally by F. C. Williams and his team at the Telecommunications Research Establishment (now the

Royal Radar Establishment) at Malvern, Worcestershire early in 1941. The techniques involved in automatic tracking radar equipment were used later in automatic tracking optical and radio telescopes.

Another World War II development whose influence has been far-reaching was that of *systems engineering*. I like to refer to systems engineering as the systemic arts because the field embraces such a broad spectrum of human activity. For example, systems engineering is concerned with the operation of all complex systems and machines. As such it is implicit in the theory and practice of cybernetics, communication systems, operations research, econometrics (the application of mathematics and statistics to problems in economics), and human factors engineering. Automation is essentially a special branch of systems engineering.

Let us pause for a moment to consider the broader implications of the systemic arts. Perhaps the most dynamic aspect in the evolution of human society is the interaction between scientific research, technological development and social change. Social change is obviously an inevitable consequence of technological change.

As technology and society advance we must be concerned increasingly with the behaviour of the "complete system" and not merely with the behaviour of individual parts of the whole. In particular, we will be called upon to define adequately the desired goals of the process or system in which we are interested. In general, the more complex the process or system, the more complex the goals.

As an example consider a particular industry as the system under consideration. The structure of the industry consists of a hierarchy of increasingly complex units. For example, a single operation in a manufacturing plant can be regarded as an elementary component with an easily defined goal. The plant itself, involving as it does a multiplicity of interacting component operations, may be regarded as a unit with more complex goals than the individual component. A complex of plants and administrative offices, making up a single industrial organization, constitutes the next higher level of complexity and hence of goals. And the total number of organizations which together form an industrial complex may be regarded as the "system". There is a hierarchy of operations, each embracing all operational levels below it in the structure. The study of the dynamic behaviour of such systems may be regarded as a study in the systemic arts. Through the use of large digital computers as "simulators" we can study how the various components in a system interact through information feedback links and what causes undesirable fluctuating behaviour. For example, fluctuations in production, sales, etc. The types of systems which can be studied in this way are unfortunately still very elementary, although the methods and techniques at present being developed will no doubt prove valuable when we have built up enough experience to tackle the bigger problems.

The names of Blackett, Wiener, and Tustin stand out as the outstanding pioneers in the systemic arts. It was the urgent need to improve anti-aircraft defence and communication systems during World War II which focused interest on this new design philosophy. And in particular it was the advent of radar, necessitating a completely new approach to defence systems, which culminated of course in the guided missile, which triggered off systems thinking as we interpret it today. Furthermore, the fundamental ideas of human factors engineering were developed during World War II in connection with the study of man-machine systems. How do men and machines interact? I am sure that the reader will agree that living as we do in a technological environment this question may become one of the most important facing society.

And epitomizing systems thinking, and also providing a powerful tool for systems study, especially in simulating the behaviour of complicated systems, the digital computer has great potential for the future.

All in all the impact of World War II military technology on the world of today has been extraordinary. In fact, the special electronic circuits which were developed for the new radar equipments provided the basis for computer circuits. The measurement of the range of a target, using radar, is achieved by determining the time taken for a pulse, transmitted by the radar antenna, to reach the target and to be reflected back to the radar; this is essentially the measurement of a time interval. To measure a time interval of such very short duration we require very high speed counting circuits. The counting circuit can be regarded as a clock—a clock that measures time intervals of fractions of a millionth of a second. This provides an excellent illustration of how broadly based and interdependent science and technology are.

I mentioned previously the idea of studying the whole system rather than the system as a collection of sub-systems and components. This idea, first used on a widespread scale during the last war, is now one of the basic philosophies of modern industry. Management science is the term normally used to describe the application of scientific principles and the principles of systems thinking to the decision-making process. And, of course, the decisions of governments, industrial leaders, educators, etc. determine the future course of society and the future course of history—the more scientifically oriented the decision-makers are the more objective the decisions they make.

The computer is playing an increasingly important part in a variety of complex control problems. In particular it has been helpful in studying the dynamics of, for example, chemical processes, and in the analysis of statistical data relating to the control of traffic on land and in the air, and, of course, in solving complex mathematical problems which have helped engineers to design control systems. But today, in addition, the computer is frequently an integral part of the information handling system involved in complex feedback systems.

One of the most important fields of application of computer control is in the chemical industry and the petroleum industry. If we want to improve the quality of chemical products, without unduly increasing the cost of production, we find that it is necessary to change the operating conditions of the plant continually in order to ensure that it is working at optimum levels. The problems to be solved in order to achieve the best operating conditions are usually so difficult that it is necessary to use a computer "on-line"—that is, the computer is continually tied in to the chemical plant and receives a continual stream of information from both operators and instruments. If a single man, or a group of men, were to try to read a large number of instrument dials in perhaps a few seconds the task would be impossible. In addition, if he were required to compare readings with previous readings and to associate the readings of different instruments one with the other, he would quickly saturate.

Unacceptable operating delays would arise and the chemical process might be in danger. The computer is the only practicable approach to such problems.

Other interesting applications of digital computers have been concerned with the control of traffic. An air traffic control system, for example, which handles the complicated task of controlling the take-off and the landing of aircraft at a busy international airport is of increasing importance. Such a system comprises a large number of information feedback channels which carry the radar information giving target positions, meteorological data, aircraft identification, etc. The job allocated to the computer is to sort out the individual tracks of the aircraft, and their status, and to help the controller predict approximate touch-down times especially when aircraft are "stacked" in the vicinity of the airport at different heights because of poor visibility conditions. Eventually, and perhaps within the next five years, the computer will have the capability of automatically directing aircraft and landing them under low visibility conditions. Human controllers will still be required to monitor the over-all situation and to take over in case unusual or emergency situations arise. The enormous increase in air traffic, coupled with increased aircraft speeds and carrying capacities, will make it essential for airports to be equipped with powerful radar equipments and powerful computers and with the appropriate status display boards all under automatic control.

Another example of modern control technology is the numerical control of machine tools. In the cases of manually controlled machine tools the instructions to the machine operator are usually contained in a "blue-print" of the part to be machined. In the case of a numerically controlled machine tool, these instructions are all contained on a reel of magnetic tape. The sequence of operations involved can be summarized simply as follows:

(a) Convert the information contained in the drawing into a logical sequence of operations which can be described in terms of simple geometrical statements, such as, for example, "proceed in a straight line from a point with coordinates (x_1, y_1) to a point with coordinates (x_2, y_2)".

(b) The sequence of steps is converted by an operator, using a special keyboard, into coded information on a magnetic tape.

(*c*) The information on the magnetic tape provides the inputs to a special-purpose computer whose output is a master five-channel tape which controls the machine tool. Three of the channels are for the x, y and z coordinate motions respectively, the fourth channel is required to control the speed of the cutting tool, and the fifth channel is used for special instructions.

The master magnetic tape controls the table of the machine tool and the speed of the cutting tool. In fact, what happens is that at each instant of time the magnetic tape stores the required position of the table as x, y, z coordinates. The actual position of the table is determined by high precision optical measuring systems and compared with the desired coordinates. If errors exist the appropriate control motors re-position the machine-tool table to reduce the errors to zero. The accuracy of modern numerically-controlled machine tools is already greater than that achievable by human operators and the speed of carrying out the machining process is appreciably greater. In the manufacture of high-precision cams, aircraft models for wind-tunnel studies, jigs and fixtures for mass production processes, the automatically controlled tools are proving to be immensely useful. They constitute still another example of how man is utilizing the feedback principle to save himself from the boredom of performing essentially programmed tasks.

3. Measurement and Communication

All systems, physical and biological, which embody information feedback are, by their nature, sensitive in one way or another to changes in their environment. Indeed, the innate capability of man, as individual or in society, to recognize change (change in temperature, change in language, change in sound, change in water level, change in a crowd's reactions, etc.) is one of the most important characteristics he possesses. We could not live if we were unable to recognize change. Sometimes our bodies recognize change and take appropriate action without our being conscious of it. For instance, after running or carrying out heavy physical work, the body needs more oxygen than normally. A whole battery of sensors send signals to the lower brain and to a variety of reflex centres giving instructions to the respiratory system to increase the rate of breathing. The regulation of breathing depends on the sensitivity of parts of the lower brain (the so-called pons and medulla) being sensitive to changes in the acidity of the blood and to changes in carbon dioxide pressure in the respiratory system. In addition, there are pressure sensitive cells attached to the aorta, pulmonary and carotid arteries which detect minute changes in blood pressure and transmit, through nerve fibres, feedback signals to the control centres in the brain.

When we talk about recognizing changes we generally refer to such common situations as changing weather, or changing timetables, or changing governments, etc. But we must, in addition, regard the recognition of change as the first step in initiating the control of a process, or the behaviour of our bodies. The important point to note is that any significant change in our environment, or in a machine's behaviour, or in our health, leads to action in one form or another. It is not difficult to extend the argument and to conclude that fundamental in all feedback control systems is a capability of recognizing change.

Usually recognition, in the sense of detection, of change is accompanied by a capability of measuring the magnitude of the change, and a capability of communicating this information to a control centre where steps can be initiated to take the appropriate correcting action. We say that the information relating to the change in, for example, the physical quantity being measured is fed back to the control centre.

When we carry out scientific experiments, we measure the values of important variables, such as temperature, distance, light intensity, etc. and we use the results to test some theory or hypothesis. Measurement is not only a basic characteristic of scientific research but it comes into almost every aspect of life itself. Lord Kelvin, the 19th century British scientist, was so convinced of the importance of measurement that he propounded what has become known as the "Kelvin Dictum". Kelvin wrote,

"When you can measure what you are speaking of and express it in numbers you know that on which you are discoursing. But if you cannot measure it and express it in numbers, your knowledge is of a very meagre and unsatisfactory kind."

In spite of the rather unusual wording of the dictum its significance, especially in the field of control, cannot be overemphasized. Perhaps we can regard the Kelvin dictum as one of the unwritten "laws" of science and engineering.

Initially, we must consider a basic question. In order to control a given process or system, what quantities must be measured? An important point to note is that in most processes the controlling, or regulating, of the value of a particular variable is not an end in itself. We must distinguish between the control variable, which is the variable we measure and regulate, on the one hand, and the object variable, or condition, which describes the ultimate object of the control operation, on the other. Usually the object variable is not easy to measure, hence the introduction of a control variable. For instance, in the control of a nuclear reactor, as mentioned in Chapter 1, the control variable is the neutron flux density within the reactor core, and the object variable is the power output of the reactor. As a second example consider the domestic thermostat. The control variable is room temperature (e.g. the desired value is set on the dial of a thermostat) and the object variable is personal comfort. The latter depends not only on room temperature but on such factors as humidity and air motion. The most convenient variable to control is clearly temperature. As a third example, consider the problem of controlling a chemical process. The process may be a plant for the manufacture of, say, ammonia. To achieve the desired quality of the final product (quality can be regarded as the "object variable") it is necessary to maintain the pressure of the chemical reaction at a pre-set value—in this example pressure is a control variable (there may be others). By measuring continually the pressure in the reaction chamber, and by feeding back this value and comparing it with the desired value, we obtain the so-called error signal which is used to actuate the automatic control system.

When we talk about measurement our thoughts immediately turn to instruments. The term "instrumentation" as used by control engineers and space technologists, relates, for instance, to

(a) the measurement of controlled variables (temperature, voltage, etc.),
(b) the transmission of data,
(c) the conversion of one form of energy to another (e.g. the conversion of electrical energy to mechanical energy as carried out by an electric motor), and
(d) the conversion of one kind of coded data to another kind (as discussed at the end of this chapter).

When we refer to communication of information we are concerned with telephone lines, radio channels, or perhaps hydraulic or pneumatic transmission systems in which the oil pressure or air pressure varies in accordance with the message we wish to communicate. Measurement and communication are inseparable operations in the sense that unless there is a means of communicating the measured value to a human being, perhaps by means of a light ray, or to an automatic controller, there would be no point in carrying out the measurement process. Later in this chapter we will consider some common forms of communication system. For the time being we will examine in some detail the measurement process.

The instruments we are interested in can be regarded as special classes of energy conversion devices. For instance, the measurement of temperature usually involves the extracting of a small quantity of heat from the process or system whose temperature is required. And this actuates a simple conversion system, which we identify as the instrument. The latter converts the small quantity of heat energy into, in the case of a gas or liquid thermometer, mechanical energy because the heat causes expansion of the liquid or gas, and we assume this expansion is proportional to the heat extracted. In another well-known system the heat energy is converted into electrical energy by using a simple thermocouple, which, when heated, gives rise to an electric current which flows across the junction of two unlike metals.

Several important characteristics apply to all measuring devices. The first is that, in the measurement of temperature, for example, heat energy is transferred from the process to the measuring instrument as long as there is a temperature difference between the process and the instrument. When the temperatures are the same there is, ideally, no transfer of energy between the two (I say ideally because, in fact, there will be a continuous interchange of energy between process and instrument but the net transfer will be virtually zero). The total heat energy transferred can be regarded as proportional to the temperature difference between the process and the thermometer at the time the measuring operation was started.

It is particularly important to note that during measurement the transfer of energy is not carried out instantaneously. A finite time is required—this is called an instrumental time-delay and, as we will see subsequently, it may take a variety of forms. As a result of the time-delay inherent in all measuring processes, we distinguish between the *static accuracy* of an instrument and its *dynamic accuracy*. If, for instance, we measure the temperature of a liquid in a large insulated tank into which no energy flows, the thermometer reading will eventually reach a so-called steady-state and the difference between the actual temperature of the liquid and the temperature as indicated by the thermometer gives a measure of the "static accuracy" of the instrument. On the other hand, if we measure continuously the temperature of liquid flowing along a pipe, when the temperature of the liquid is continually fluctuating, the thermometer reading will always be trying to "catch up", so to speak. As a result the temperature as recorded by the thermometer is rarely the same as the actual temperature. In practice, in all biological systems, and in the majority of physical and chemical processes, that which we measure is usually changing and this means that our biological sensors, and our physical instruments, must be designed to respond to change as rapidly as possible. I will illustrate the effect of time-delays on measurement later in this chapter.

Before leaving this general discussion of the measurement process, there is another important factor which should be mentioned. Since energy must be extracted from a process in order to determine its behaviour, the mere act of measurement gives rise to a change in the system which is being studied. Usually this change is insignificant but it is important to bear in mind. Its most fundamental manifestation is Heisenberg's Uncertainty Principle which states that it is impossible, at a given instant of time, to measure accurately both the position and the momentum of a fundamental particle—this is a basic law of nature which in crude language means that whenever we try to measure something we change it. But don't be too alarmed about this because as I mentioned before in the vast majority of cases the change is infinitesimal. However, if I insert a large cold mercury thermometer in a small test-tube containing hot liquid, it is obvious that I will be affecting the temperature of the liquid because I am using a crude and non-scientific method of measurement.

We turn now to a rather more quantitative approach to the question of time-delays in instruments, and incidentally in processes.

The Dynamic Characteristics of Instruments

The process of measurement can be illustrated in simple block diagram form as shown in Fig. 10, in which:

x_i = actual value of physical variable,

x_o = measured value of physical variable.

If we are interested in the temperature of the process, the instrument may be a thermocouple coupled to a milli-ammeter, or a bi-metallic strip as in the domestic thermostat, etc. In some instruments there is a finite time-delay between a change in the magnitude of a physical variable and the corresponding response of the instrument. It is worthy of record that the human being when operating as an instrument or as a control system involves such a time-delay. It is called human reaction-time and will be considered in Chapter 4.

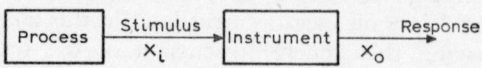

Fig. 10. Process of measurement

In general, an instrument with an inherent finite-time delay responds to a stimulus as shown in Fig. 11. Letting the actual value of the variable being measured be x_i and the measured

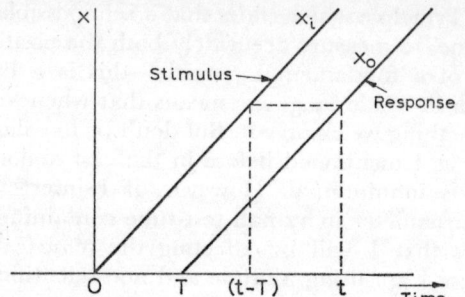

Fig. 11. Response of system characterized by finite time-delay

value of the variable be x_o, the simple algebraic relationship which exists between x_o and x_i can be expressed by the following equation:

$$x_o(t + T) = x_i(t)$$
or
$$x_o(t) = x_i(t - T)$$

In ordinary language this means that the measured value of the variable (say, temperature) at time t is equal to the actual value of the variable at time $(t - T)$, which means that the measured value corresponds to the actual value which existed T seconds in the past.

We turn now to a more common class of instrument delay—that is, more common from the standpoint of information feedback control systems. In practice the delay characteristics inherent in biological sensors and in many physical and chemical instruments are usually complex. But for convenience in studying such systems we frequently use approximations such as the finite time-delay characteristic considered previously or the exponential time-delay characteristic to be considered next.

When a clinical thermometer is inserted in my mouth it does not give an instantaneous indication of my body temperature (assumed to be the same as my mouth temperature). The behaviour of the thermometer is illustrated in Fig. 12. At the

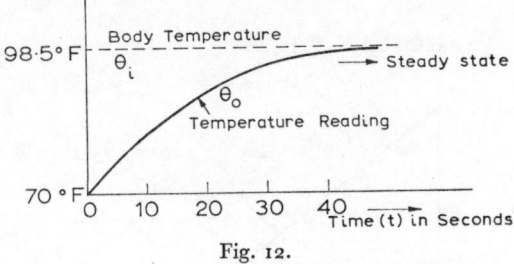

Fig. 12.

instant of insertion heat begins to flow into the bulb of the thermometer at a rate proportional to the difference in temperature between my body and the thermometer itself. As this difference decreases, so also does the rate of change of the thermometer reading until, in the limit, there is no difference in temperature between my body and the thermometer bulb—no energy is being transferred. We say that the thermometer has reached a steady-state.

The dynamic behaviour of measuring instruments is of fundamental importance in all branches of science and engineering. It is of particular importance in the study of information feedback systems. The response of a simple instrument subsequent to the sudden application of an input signal (we call it a "step" function) can be described in terms of the "law of exponential growth (or decay)". In Fig. 12, the response of the thermometer is exponential in form. If we plot, for example, $\log (\theta_i - \theta_o)$

as a function of time (t) we find that the resulting graph is a straight line as shown in Fig. 13. This implies that the value of $(\theta_i - \theta_o)$ decreases exponentially with time. Such behaviour is characteristic of an instrument, or system, when the *rate* of response is proportional to the difference between the level of stimulation (θ_i) and the level of response (θ_o) at time t. Written symbolically:

$$\dot{\theta}_o = \frac{1}{T}(\theta_i - \theta_o)$$

where $\dot{\theta}_o$ represents the time-rate of change of θ_o, and T is a constant described as the time constant.

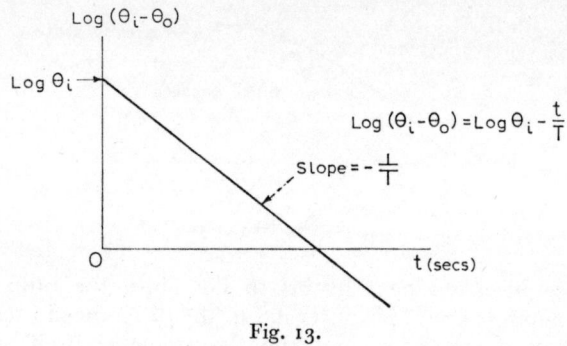

Fig. 13.

The exponential law of decay applies also to the decay of radio-active substances. In this case the number of radio-active nuclei disintegrating each second (i.e. the rate of decay) is proportional to the number of radio-active nuclei actually present in the sample.

Many examples of instruments with exponential delay characteristics exist and it is not easy to choose an appropriate one for detailed study. However, in view of the importance of the instruments used in the measurement of electrical quantities, for example, the ammeter and the voltmeter, they are worthy of special consideration.

If an electrical voltage is applied across the terminals of a well-damped voltmeter, the subsequent behaviour of the instrument, assuming a coil with negligible mass, is as shown in Fig. 14. At the instant of application, or, perhaps more accurately, after a small delay due to the time taken for electric current to build up in the deflection coil of the instrument, the rate of the angular deflection of the pointer is a maximum because the restoring torque exerted by the helical spring is negligible. But as the pointer moves across the scale it slows down because the resulting deflecting torque (that is, the electro-magnetic torque minus the torque exerted by the spring) is continually reduced until finally the pointer comes to rest when the two opposing torques are equal in magnitude. Compare the behaviour of the voltmeter with that of the thermometer considered previously.

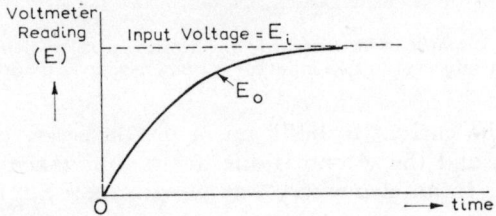

Fig. 14. Response of a damped voltmeter (mass of coil and pointer neglected)

The question, "How long does it take for the instrument to reach a steady-state when the reading of the pointer corresponds closely to the value of the applied voltage?" is often of great importance in experimental work and especially when the voltmeter reading provides the feedback signal in an automatic control system. For example, if the mass of the suspended coil is not negligible, if the spring of the voltmeter is stiff, and if the damping effect is not appreciable, the sudden application of a voltage across the input terminals may give rise to oscillatory behaviour of the pointer as indicated in Fig. 15. If there is no damping present the subsequent behaviour of the pointer would be an undamped oscillation as shown dotted. Oscillatory behaviour of this kind in an instrument, or in a control system element, is usually undesirable because of the uncertainty involved in the measuring process. For instance, it is well known by designers of instruments and control systems that if high speeds of response are sought there is an increased probability of oscillatory behaviour—we will look into this in Chapter 6.

Sometimes a sequence of exponential delays arises in the operation of a single instrument. For instance, in the case of the voltmeter two delays can be identified, the first is due to the time

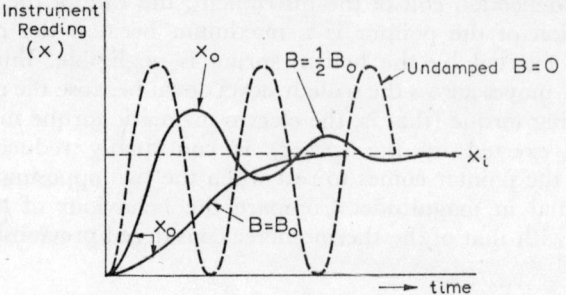

Fig. 15. Response of instrument (e.g. voltmeter, accelerometer, etc.) when subjected to step input for varying degrees of damping

taken for the current to build up in the deflection coil of the instrument, and the second is due to the time taken to deflect the pointer. In an elementary way we can represent sequential

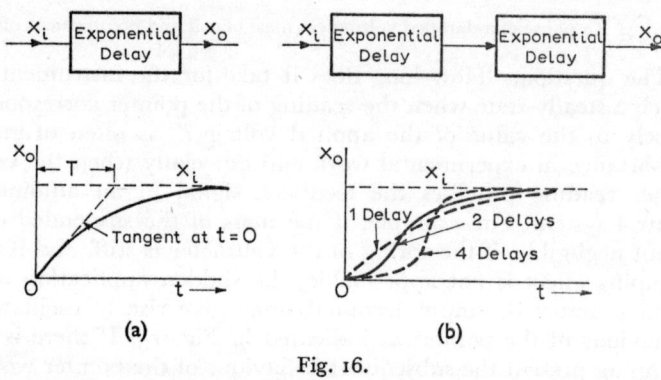

Fig. 16.

time delays as "blocks" as shown in Fig. 16(a) and (b). In case (a) the instrument has a single exponential lag and the response is the usual simple exponential law. In case (b) the instrument embodies two exponential lags in series, and the extra lag causes a slowing down of the response of the instrument as shown in the accompanying graph. When three or four exponential lags are present the slowing down of the response is still further accentuated. One of the main tasks of the instrument designer is to minimize the number of exponential delays involved in his instrument and also to minimize the "time-constants" of those which have to be tolerated.

The time-constant of a simple measuring instrument, embodying a single exponential lag, can best be determined experimentally by plotting the response of the instrument after the sudden application of an input signal. If the tangent to the response curve is obtained at $t = 0$, the time when the input signal is applied, this tangent intersects the steady-state value line x_i as shown in Fig. 16(a) where T is the time-constant of the instrument. The diagram suggests that the larger the value of T the slower the response of the instrument.

Principle of an Accelerometer

One of the key instruments in determining the dynamic behaviour of a rocket during the launching period is the accelerometer. Its principle is based on Newton's Second and Third Laws of Motion.

Figure 17 illustrates the principle of the vertical accelerometer. It is assumed that the position of the mass m can be measured as a voltage (using, for example, a linear potentiometer) and that this voltage can be transmitted to the space vehicle computer control unit and also to the ground control centre.

In the rest position, when the vertical acceleration is zero, the mass m is in the datum position shown; the displacement is zero. The mass is acted upon by two forces—its weight, $W = mg$, acts vertically downwards, and an equal force W exerted by the spring acts vertically upwards. The instrument in the zero rest position, is represented in Fig. 17(a).

Now suppose, through the thrust exerted by the rocket motors, the rocket lifts off the launching pad with a uniform acceleration of f ft./sec./sec. The mass m is now acted upon by a force, acting vertically downwards, which is equal to $m(f + g)$. This force, being greater than the combined upward forces due to the spring, and the friction which is developed between the cylinder of mass m and the walls of the accelerometer case when there is relative motion between them, causes m to be accelerated vertically downwards relative to the accelerometer case. Subsequently, the mass m will achieve a maximum velocity (downward) relative to the case, and will then begin to slow down because the combined forces acting vertically upwards are greater than the force acting vertically downwards. At a still later time the mass m will be brought to rest relative to the accelerometer case and at that time

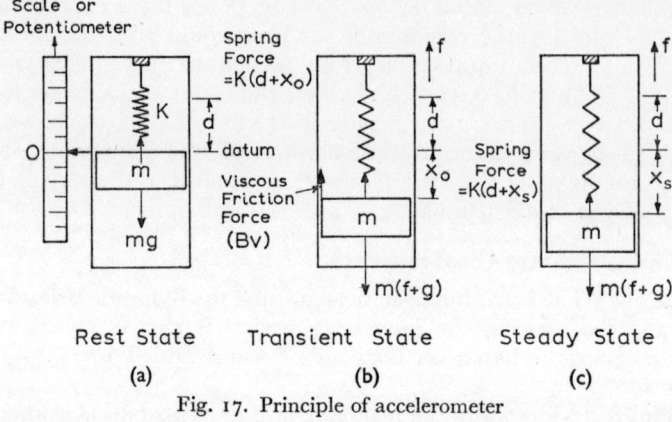

Fig. 17. Principle of accelerometer

its displacement from the datum position, say x_s, gives a measure of the vertical acceleration of the system. In the steady-state position shown in Fig. 17(c), there is no relative motion between m and the case and hence no friction force acts. In this state of dynamic equilibrium the force exerted by the spring is just balanced by the inertial force $m(f+g)$. Assuming the force exerted by the spring is proportional to the extension of the spring (Hooke's Law) we can write the steady-state equation as:

$$K(x_s + d) = m(f + g) \qquad (1)$$

where K is the spring constant and d is the extension of the spring due to m when $f = 0$. But in the rest position, corresponding to zero vertical acceleration of the system, the force-balance equation is:

$$Kd = mg \qquad (2)$$

and hence, by subtracting equation (2) from equation (1) we obtain:

$$Kx_s = mf$$

and therefore

$$f = \frac{Kx_s}{m}$$

Since K is assumed to be constant and m is constant, the displacement x_s of the mass is proportional to the vertical acceleration of the rocket.

It is important that we should examine the dynamics of the accelerometer in more detail. In particular, I intend to regard the behaviour of the accelerometer as being typical of a wide range of instruments, and even of such devices as electrical motors and hydraulic motors. Of special interest is the so-called *transient behaviour* of the instrument (see Fig. 17(*b*))—that is, its behaviour, starting from a state of rest, subsequent to the application of a sudden change in acceleration. In the example of the accelerometer, because of the thrust of the rocket motors, the instrument is subjected to a "sudden" increase* in acceleration from zero to f ft./sec./sec. Eventually, as we have seen, the instrument achieves a steady-state in the sense that there is no relative motion between the mass m and the case of the accelerometer which is, of course, attached to the framework of the rocket. And, obviously, a period of time elapses between the application of the accelerating thrust and the instrument achieving a steady-state. What happens during this period is of considerable interest.

It is worthwhile at this point to define more rigorously the three important forces which act on the accelerometer mass m during the transient state (when there is relative motion between mass and case). These forces are:

(i) the "spring force", in which the force acting on the cylinder is proportional to the linear displacement of the spring as shown in Fig. 18(*a*);
(ii) the "viscous friction force", which is proportional to the relative velocity between mass and case as shown diagrammatically in Fig. 18(*b*);

---

* "Sudden" is, of course, a relative term. It is used here to describe an approximation to the "step function".

(iii) the "inertia force", which when acting on a body causes uniform acceleration—it is represented diagrammatically in Fig. 18(c).

Note with (i) that a constant force, say F, produces a constant displacement, say x; with (ii) that a constant force F produces, in the steady-state after the acceleration has been reduced to zero, a constant velocity, say v; and with (iii) that a constant force

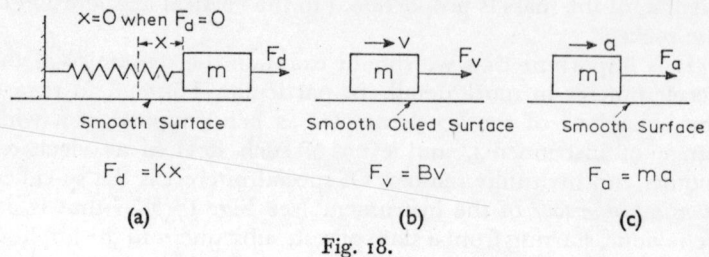

Fig. 18.

F causes a mass m to accelerate with a constant acceleration, say a. The relationships can be written algebraically as follows:

(i) Force proportional to linear displacement;

$$F_d = Kx$$

in which K is the spring constant which is defined as the force per unit linear displacement of the spring.

(ii) Force proportional to linear velocity;

$$F_v = Bv$$

in which B is the viscous friction coefficient which is defined as the force per unit linear relative velocity between, say, m and the case.

(iii) Force proportional to linear acceleration;

$$F_a = ma$$

in which m is the mass of the body upon which the force is acting.

We are now in a position to study the dynamic behaviour of the accelerometer. We note first that, in addition to the force acting on the mass m due to gravity (i.e. $W = mg$), if the accelerometer case is accelerated upwards with uniform acceleration, f ft./sec./sec., a vertical force (mf) acts downwards on the mass m. This follows from Newton's Third Law of Motion, i.e. action and reaction forces are equal and opposite. Another way of looking at the problem is to regard the case as stationary, then the relative acceleration of m would be f acting downwards.

But this force, mf, tending to pull the mass m in a downwards direction relative to the case* must, for dynamic equilibrium,

(i) accelerate the mass m vertically downwards with acceleration "a" relative to the case—this requires a force ma,
(ii) provide a force adequate to overcome the viscous friction force (between mass and case) which, if the velocity of the mass relative to the case is v, is a force Bv,
(iii) when the velocity of the mass is v, and its acceleration is "a", provide a force to displace the mass through a distance x_o, this force is Kx_o, where x_o is the displacement from the datum position.

Reference should be made to Fig. 17(b) remembering that $mg = Kd$.

For dynamic equilibrium we can write,

$$ma + Bv + Kx_o = mf,$$

in which we assume that at $t = 0$, $v = 0$, and $x_o = 0$.

If we introduce the notation of the differential calculus and recall that acceleration is the time-rate of change of velocity, and velocity is the time-rate of change of displacement, we can replace "a" by d^2x_o/dt^2 and we can write $v = dx_o/dt$.

The equation of motion of the system may then be written,

$$m \frac{d^2x_o}{dt^2} + B \frac{dx_o}{dt} + Kx_o = mf$$

or, $$m\ddot{x}_o + B\dot{x}_o + Kx_o = mf$$

This equation is called a second order ordinary linear differential equation. When we are given the initial values of

---

* The effect of this force is very noticeable when we carry a heavy bag on an elevator. When the elevator accelerates upwards the bag "feels heavier". When the elevator decelerates, as the required floor is approached, the bag "feels lighter". And vice versa when the elevator is descending.

x_o and dx_o/dt at $t = 0$ (in the present example and in many other examples these initial values are zero) we can solve this equation for x_o. In the case of the accelerometer we have assumed that the system is accelerated suddenly and since, as we showed previously, x_s is proportional to f we can regard the input variable applied to the system as a sudden step input of displacement. We shall assume that solutions of the equation can be obtained and we consider a few special cases.

If, for example, the viscous friction coefficient (B) is zero, the equation of motion of the mass corresponds to the well-known equation of simple harmonic motion. In the example of the accelerometer, when the instrument is subjected to a suddenly applied vertical thrust which is assumed ideally to cause immediately uniform acceleration of the system, the effect on the mass, assuming no friction, is that it will be subjected to undamped oscillations. Another way of looking at it is to consider the point of suspension of a spring-supported mass to be suddenly moved vertically. Of course, the mass bounces up and down with a period which depends on the spring coefficient (K) and the mass (m). A spring with large K (i.e. a stiff spring) and a small mass will give rise to low period oscillations while a low K spring and a large m will give rise to comparatively long-period oscillations.

Clearly an accelerometer which never settles down to a steady-state is not a useful measuring instrument. In practice, we introduce viscous friction to damp out the oscillations. Many ways of introducing viscous friction are possible, the most common being the simple piston-cylinder damper and the eddy-current damper. We choose a value for B which gives adequate damping combined with a reasonably short settling time. The behaviour of the accelerometer when subjected to a suddenly applied external force for two values of the viscous friction coefficient (B) is shown in Fig. 15. The response is identical in form to that of the voltmeter and many other instruments. The value of B which produces the critically damped condition is, say $B = B_o$. *Critical damping* is achieved with the smallest value of B which gives rise to no overshoot in the response. When $B = \frac{1}{2}B_o$ it will be noted that there is appreciable overshoot during the first period of the oscillation but subsequently this is damped out as shown. In order to achieve high initial speed of response of the system, as required in many instruments, and components used in the design of automatic control systems, we usually select a value of B that is somewhat smaller than that required to give critical damping—in practice a value of B equal to approximately $\frac{3}{4}B_o$ is about optimum.

Data Transmission

An information feedback link usually involves both measurement and the transmission of the measured data to the central controller (or in the case of a simple single-loop control system to the error-measuring device). Many types of data transmission channels are known. For example, data can be transmitted by means of a shaft rotation, or by pressure variations in a hydraulic or pneumatic pipe, or electrically. The transmission of electrical signals is generally the most convenient and certainly the most flexible because line and radio links can be used.

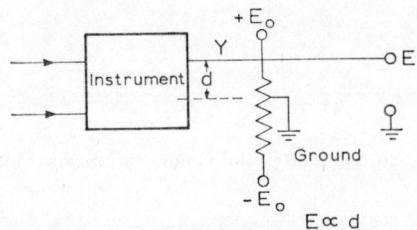

Fig. 19. Conversion of mechanical displacement 'd' into a voltage signal

Suppose we measure a particular variable, say acceleration or temperature, and obtain the measurement as a pointer displacement. This displacement, which may be linear or angular, may readily be converted into an equivalent electrical signal by using a simple potentiometer. In Fig. 19 we assume that the wiper of the potentiometer, marked Y, is attached to the output pointer of the measuring instrument. The voltage E is then the equivalent of the measured variable. If the data has to be transmitted over long distances we might have an arrangement as shown in Fig. 20. Here two potentiometers are involved. The input to the system is the position of the measuring instrument pointer Y, and, as before, this positions the wiper of potentiometer I. A human operator moves the output wiper, that is, the wiper of potentiometer II, until there is no potential difference across the voltmeter V shown in the diagram. When this happens we say that the input and output shafts are in alignment. This simple potentiometer data transmission system becomes a servomechanism if the output shaft Z is positioned automatically by a motor actuated by the potential difference across the voltmeter V. We will deal with servomechanisms in the next chapter.

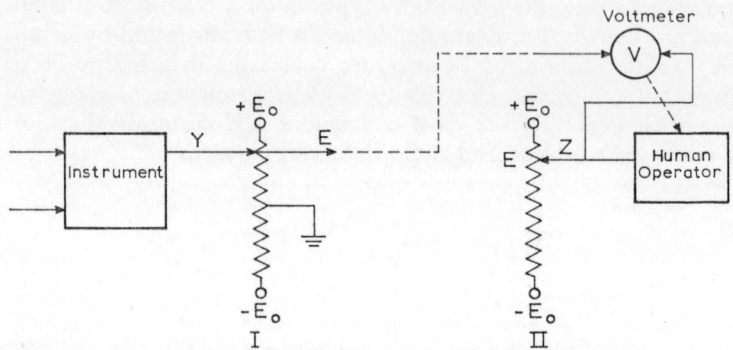

Fig. 20. An electrical d.c. data transmission link

One of the most widely used data transmission systems is the so-called "synchro system". It has many advantages over the direct-current system. Synchros are essentially small alternating-current motors or generators. They were first used during World War II in anti-aircraft fire control systems, on land, on warships, and in aircraft for transmitting data relating to the position and speed of ships and aircraft targets. Their applications throughout industry and in the space programme are widespread. Since it is not my purpose in this book to give detailed descriptions of specialized instruments and components, I will merely illustrate two important synchro arrangements.

Consider the data transmission system shown schematically in Fig. 21. Both the input and the output of the system are mechanical shaft rotations. The rotor of the synchro-generator (transmitter) is connected to an a.c. reference voltage as shown.

Voltages are then induced in the three stator windings of the generator so that the magnitudes and polarities of these induced voltages are uniquely determined by the position of the input shaft x_i which is connected to the rotor. If this three-phase a.c. output is now used to energize the corresponding stator windings of the synchro-motor (receiver), and if the rotor of the synchro-motor is energized by the a.c. reference voltage then the rotor of the synchro-motor, which is connected to the output shaft x_o, will set itself in alignment with the input, or generator, shaft.

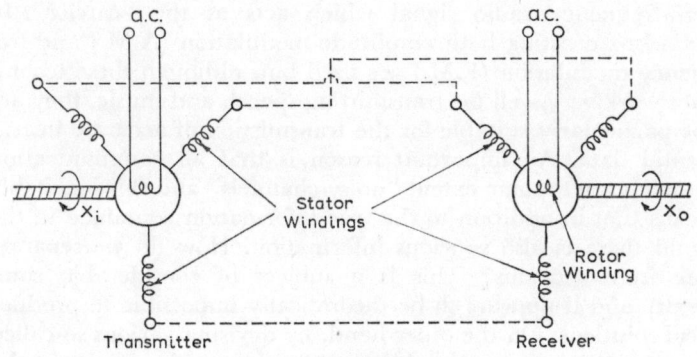

Fig. 21. A synchro data link

If, of course, the output shaft is loaded then misalignments between the input and output shafts are inevitable. A synchro system that combines data transmission and the determination of the misalignment between an input and an output shaft and which generates a voltage whose amplitude is proportional to the misalignment will be considered in Chapter 4.

In the data transmission systems we have considered, lines of communication in the form of current-carrying conductors are needed. Obviously, in the ground control of unmanned space vehicles, or in the transmission of data from a satellite to earth, it is impossible to use line communications. The problem of accurately transmitting data from the instruments of a space vehicle to earth is one of great complexity and much beyond our present scope. But a brief introduction to the subject is perhaps in order because of its tremendous importance in the whole space programme, and indeed in many other programmes. For instance, it was announced recently that automatic remote monitoring of the hearts of patients, fitted with artificial valves, and other apparatus for relieving the human heart, when the patients are carrying out their normal employment, is now possible. The electro-cardiograms are recorded remotely and checked by medical scientists.

The common method of transmitting information over a radio channel is by causing the data to "modulate a carrier signal". This means that we superimpose our message on a very high-frequency radio signal which acts as the "carrier". In radio broadcasting both amplitude modulation (A.M.) and frequency modulation (F.M.) are used but, although these techniques work very well for transmitting speech and music, they are not particularly suitable for the transmission of accurate instrumental data. An important reason is that all communication channels are to some extent "noisy channels" and this inevitably means that in addition to the true information contained in the signal there is also spurious information. How do we separate true from spurious? This is a subject of considerable complexity and it appears to be theoretically impossible to produce ideal solutions. On the other hand, by devising various so-called coding techniques and adding redundancy, for example, by repeating the message many times, we can achieve a reasonable degree of accuracy.

One method which lends itself very well to space communications problems is to "digitalize" the information to be transmitted and to transmit it, for example, in the form of a binary digital code, i.e. one that uses only the figures 0 and 1, which are very easy to represent electrically.

When the information to be transmitted is in the form of a continuous signal which may, for example, give a measure of electron density in the ionosphere, it is necessary to sample periodically the data as illustrated in Fig. 22. Obviously, the smaller the sampling period the more accurate the sampling process—if the time between successive samples is infinitesimally small the sampled data and the continuous data may be regarded as identical.

Referring to Fig. 22, we assume that each sampled data signal, $a, b, c, \ldots$, can be represented by a binary number. (For example, if $a = 17$ units its binary equivalent is 10001.*) The signal can be represented as a sequence of pulses as shown in Fig. 23—it is

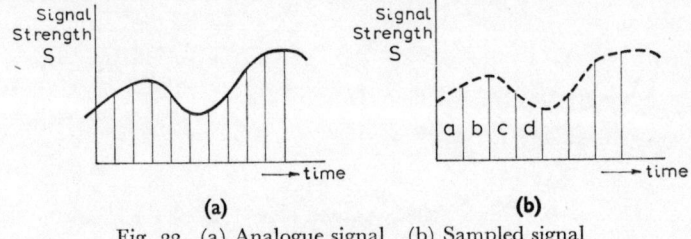

Fig. 22. (a) Analogue signal   (b) Sampled signal

convenient, for practical purposes, to let each "binary word", representing each sample, have an equal number of binary digits.

The effects of "noise" can be minimized by:

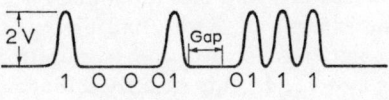

Fig. 23. Binary signals

(i) assuming a "1" occurs at a given point if the signal voltage is greater than, say, V volts, and assuming a "0" if the signal amplitude is less than V volts—see Fig. 23,
(ii) triplicating each communication channel and using at each point the "majority evidence" (if, say, channels I and II indicate a "1" and channel III a "0", we decide on a "1"),
(iii) introducing additional check digits into the message.

We consider now a simple binary coding system. Suppose the data to be transmitted is in the form of the angular displacement (i.e. rotation) of a mechanical spindle—perhaps the pointer spindle of a simple instrument. A "pattern plate", engraved with a binary code, shown in Fig. 24, is attached to the spindle and in fact replaces the pointer. Sensitive brushes,

* That is $1 \times 2^4 + 0 \times 2^3 + 0 \times 2^2 + 0 \times 2^1 + 1 \times 2^0 = 16 + 0 + 0 + 0 + 1 = 17$.

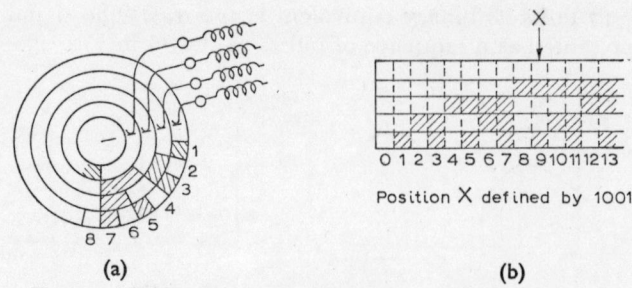

Fig. 24. (a) Circular binary pattern plate (b) Linear binary pattern plate

as shown, collect the information which is transmitted in the form of binary words as demonstrated previously.

If necessary, the binary information, perhaps received over a satellite communication channel, can be processed by a computer, or it can be reconverted into analogue form. The information can also be compared with that desired, and a binary coded correction signal generated and transmitted to correct the behaviour of the system. In this case the binary coded information from the satellite is essentially feedback information and a closed loop system is involved in the control operation.

4. Servomechanisms

A new word in our vocabulary, whose use has burgeoned in the flood tide of modern science and technology, is the word "servo". It is the abbreviated form of the word "servomechanism". For instance, in some countries cars are said to be fitted with "servo-assisted brakes" and "servo-assisted steering"—in North America the corresponding terms are power-brakes and power-steering. The latter usage gives us a clue concerning the nature of servomechanisms or servo systems. Actually the term "servo" is derived from a Greek word which means "slave", and as we might guess a servomechanism behaves in a slave-like manner—its output member is constrained to repeat the motion of an input member at an increased power level. A formal definition of the term reads something like this:

"A servomechanism is an automatic feedback control system in which the motion of an output member (e.g. the output shaft) is constrained to follow closely the motion of an input member, and in which power amplification is incorporated."

The behaviour of a servomechanism is similar to that of an automatic regulator or a feedback electronic amplifier, and a common theoretical treatment applies. However, a regulator (e.g. temperature regulator or thermostat) differs from a servomechanism insofar as the goal of a regulator is to keep the value of the controlled variable constant, whereas the goal of a servomechanism is to constrain the output of the controlled system to follow the input.

A good example of a servomechanism is the system which automatically controls the position of the rudder of a large ship. In controlling the heading of the ship the helmsman exerts a comparatively small torque (torque is the moment of a force, i.e. force times distance about, say, the axis of the helmsman's wheel). The rudder is positioned by the operation of a servomechanism—the position of the helm is the input to the servo and the position of the rudder is the output. Clearly, appreciable power amplification is needed when we consider the massive size of the rudders of some ships and the forces which must be exerted to move them.

Normally the term servomechanism applies to so-called position control systems. We may, for instance, remotely control the linear or angular displacement of an output shaft connected to a ship's rudder, or a control surface of a rocket or aircraft, or the cutting tool of a machine-tool, etc. But sometimes the term is used to describe systems in which the displacement of an input shaft, or knob, or joystick, controls the angular rate of rotation of the output shaft. For instance, the control of certain aircraft control-surfaces is carried out using velocity control and, similarly, some of the controls used in large cranes are of this kind. The operator displaces his "stick" to the right, or to the left, in order to control the rate of angular traverse of the crane in one sense or the other.

I am devoting a chapter to servomechanisms because of the important part they have played in the development of all classes of feedback control systems in particular and of cybernetics in general. There are two reasons for this. In the first place—compared with the majority of biological control systems and the complex control systems used in chemical plants, servomechanisms are comparatively simple devices and lend themselves naturally to mathematical analysis. And secondly, servomechanisms were needed in such large numbers during World War II that their development proceeded rapidly and, in general, was based on sound mathematical and scientific principles. It was also servomechanism theory that first stimulated Norbert Wiener to develop the basic concepts of cybernetics. Their importance in the whole field of control has certainly not diminished.

Before considering the anatomy of a typical servomechanism, it is worth listing the reasons why human operators must, for the efficient operation of many industrial processes and machines, be replaced by servos.

The obvious reason for introducing automatic control is in systems where it is physically impossible for a human operator to carry out a given task because of his power and speed limitations, or because of the presence of harmful radiations or high temperatures, or the inaccessible location of the system. For example, at the present stage of development of space science and technology, manned space flights to the other planets are not yet feasible and automatic control is absolutely essential. But there are other important reasons why a human operator may be unsuitable as an element in a control system; some of these are:

(a) In systems where high speeds of response are essential, the effect of human reaction time prohibits the application of correction signals with adequate speed. For a normal human being, reaction time is of the order of 0·3 seconds and this may be prohibitive in high-speed systems.
(b) Manual control of many laboratory experiments and industrial processes, which require continuous and accurate control over long periods of time, is usually undesirable. Human operators are subject to physical fatigue and to the effects of boredom which eventually cause deterioration of performance. And if, in addition, the operator is subjected to mental stress while operating a system we would expect a falling-off of efficiency.
(c) Modern synchros, amplifiers, and servo motors are capable of a level of precision appreciably higher than that achievable by human operators.
(d) Unless very simple tasks are undertaken it is not possible to standardize the behaviour of human operators. Accordingly, the design of control systems in which human beings are involved is often based on unacceptable tolerances. However, in some control systems—space vehicles are an example—operations may be required which call for human judgement. In such systems the presence of human operators is essential.
(e) From a strictly economic point of view it is frequently uneconomical to use human operators when they can be effectively replaced by servo systems. The point is that if a man can be replaced by a servo system, he is carrying out a low-level task for which human intelligence is not required, and this is wasteful of human resources.

In view of the important part played by man in controlling machines such as cars, aircraft, machine tools, etc. we will devote some space, later in this chapter, to examining manual control situations which, because they embody information feedback channels and power amplification, can be regarded as a special class of servos. But first we will consider the nature of the sequence of operations which make up a servo system.

Elements of a Servomechanism

Servo systems are normally designated as mechanical, electrical, hydraulic, or pneumatic systems. However, in practice, servo systems frequently embody mechanical, electrical, hydraulic, etc. components and can be regarded as hybrid systems. For example, electro-hydraulic servo systems are used widely in the control of aircraft control surfaces, and in machine tool controls. These systems usually incorporate electrical data-transmission systems of the type we discussed in the last chapter. Since hydraulic and pneumatic servos are not easy to describe because they incorporate unusual elements, for our present purpose, it is preferable to restrict the discussion to electrical servomechanisms. A typical a.c. electrical servomechanism is shown in Fig. 25. Its basic elements can be identified as:

(a) The synchro elements ($C.T.$ and $T.$) for the measurement of angular position of the input and output shafts and measurement of the misalignment between these shafts. This requires a special synchro system the operation of which will be considered briefly below. The synchro system also incorporates the data transmission link (F) which can be identified as the information feedback of the system. In this particular case the information fed back takes the form of a three-phase a.c. signal.

(b) A stabilizing network (N) whose purpose is to "shape" the behaviour of the system so that it is free from oscillatory behaviour but has sufficiently high speed of response. In Chapter 6 we will consider the requirements for stabilization.

(c) The a.c. electronic amplifier (A) which amplifies the error signal (e). The control signal may be regarded as a "valve" which controls the flow of energy into the system. Hence the term *power-amplifying control system*.

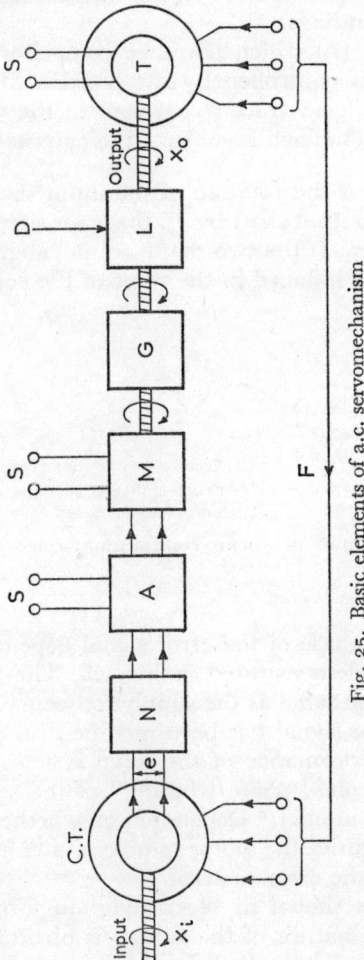

Fig. 25. Basic elements of a.c. servomechanism

(d) The servo motor (M) which obtains electrical power from an external source. Its behaviour is controlled exclusively by the amplified error signal which excites one of the two motor windings.

(e) The load (L) which normally comprises an object whose position is controlled by the position of the input shaft. Usually a gear train (G) is used in the motor-load transmission. The load is subjected to external forces (D).

If we represent the rotation of the input shaft by x_i, and the rotation of the output shaft by x_o, the error signal will, of course, be zero if $x_o = x_i$. If the two shafts are not aligned, an a.c. signal of amplitude e is induced in the rotor of the control transformer

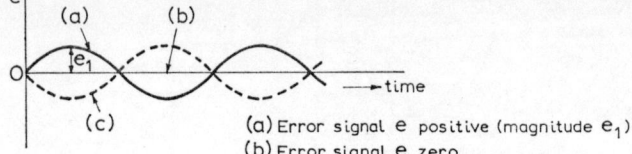

Fig. 26. Nature of synchro control transformer (c.t.) output

($C.T.$) and the phase of the error signal depends upon the sign of the error as demonstrated in Fig. 26. The frequency of the error signal is the same as the supply frequency.

After the error signal has been modified (in order to improve the dynamic performance of the servo system), and amplified, it is applied to one "phase winding" of the servo motor (a 2-phase induction motor).* Depending on whether the error signal is positive or negative the motor spindle rotates in the appropriate sense to reduce the error to zero.

The system is shown in block diagram form in Fig. 27(a). The closed-loop nature of the system is obvious. So also is the fact that power is supplied to the system from an external source so that even a very lightly loaded input shaft may control a massive load.

* The other phase winding is connected to the a.c. supply (S).

In Fig. 27(a) it will be noted that an extraneous influence (D) affects the operation of the control system. It is called the *load disturbance*. This disturbance is normally beyond our control. For example, the control surfaces of aircraft (i.e. the rudder, ailerons, etc.) are subjected to complex disturbances when the aircraft flies through turbulent air. In the example of the control of a large radio telescope antenna the effect of wind forces on the operation of the automatic control system, especially in gusty

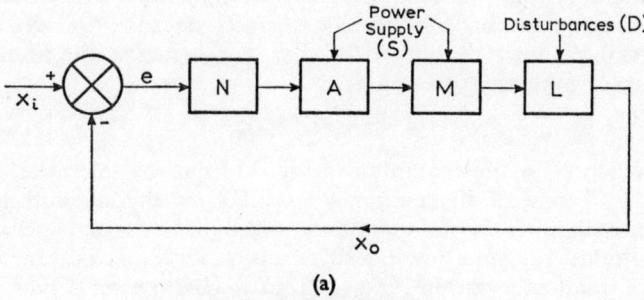

(a)

Block diagram of servomechanism

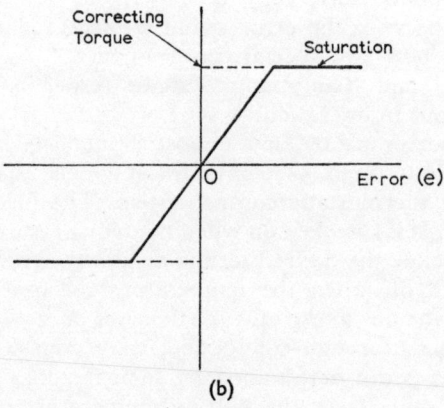

(b)

Control characteristic of continuous servo

Fig. 27.

conditions, is of prime importance. Indeed, were it not for the effect of such outside disturbances and, incidentally, variations in the voltage or frequency of the a.c. power supply, the control system would be essentially deterministic insofar as it would be possible to predict its behaviour. When the behaviour of a system is completely predictable there is no need for information feedback because a programmed sequence of controls suffices. But when external disturbances affect the operation of a control system its behaviour is to some extent uncertain. In other words the degree of system predictability decreases. In these circumstances information feedback is usually essential because the errors in "tracking" must be limited in size. For instance, the required accuracy may be expressed as,

$$|(x_i - x_o)| \leq e_m$$

in which e_m is the maximum error that can be tolerated. The left-hand side of the expression symbolizes the magnitude of the misalignment signal regardless of its sign. In normal operating conditions, e_m, for a low-power precision servomechanism, may be as small as 2 minutes of arc ($1/30°$). High-power servos may involve maximum tracking errors in the order of 15 to 30 minutes of arc.

Servomechanisms of the type shown in Fig. 25, whose behaviour will be discussed later, may be described as *continuous-control servo systems* because the error signal is measured continuously. We consider now two special classes of servos, usually referred to as "on-off" and "bang-bang" systems, respectively, which are non-continuous in operation.

On-off controls are by far the most common because they are usually simple to build. One of the most widely used is probably the domestic thermostatic control system. The furnace is either full on or off. It is switched on when the temperature of the house or office is below the desired setting on the thermostat dial, and it is switched off when the temperature reaches that desired. The ratio of the on- to the off-time depends on how much heat is lost per second, through conduction, convection and radiation. The heat losses are determined by such factors as the outside temperature (the lower the outside temperature relative to the home temperature, the greater the losses); the wind velocity and direction; and the effectiveness of the thermal insulation of the home. We generally refer to these factors as the *ambient conditions*. In fact they constitute the extraneous disturbances we talked about previously.

The elements of an on-off servo are shown in block diagram form in Fig. 28. It is perhaps not quite correct to refer to this

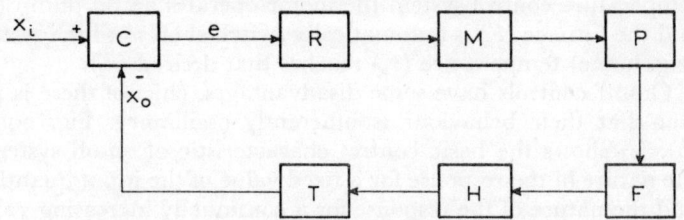

Fig. 28. Components of an on-off control system

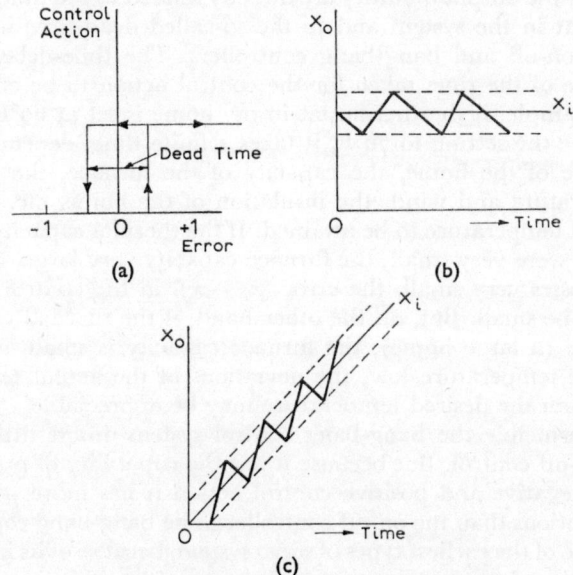

Fig. 29. Characteristics of on-off controller

system as a servo system because, in general, on-off operation is restricted to regulators in which the input is a fixed quantity. But it is convenient to introduce the idea at this stage. The error detector (C) is concerned solely with positive errors—that is, when the output quantity (x_o) has a value less than the input quantity (x_i). When this condition arises a low-power electrical signal (e) activates an electro-magnetic relay (R) whose output, at appreciably higher power, excites the motor (M) which in turn activates the process under control (P). For example, with a temperature control system the motor operates an oil pump (P) and the furnace (F) is automatically switched on until the system (e.g. home) temperature (x_o) reaches that desired (x_i).

On-off controls have some disadvantages, chief of these is the fact that their behaviour is inherently oscillatory. Fig. 29(a), (b), (c) shows the basic control characteristic of on-off systems, the nature of the response for a fixed value of the input quantity, and the nature of the response for a continually increasing value of the input quantity respectively. The amplitude of the fluctuations in the output quantity are directly related to the time-delays inherent in the system and to the so-called dead-time inherent in all on-off and bang-bang controllers. The time-delays arise because of the time taken for the control action to be effective. For example, if the thermostat in my home is set at 60°F and I increase the setting to 70°F, it takes a finite time, dependent on the size of the home, the capacity of the furnace, the outside temperature and wind, the insulation of the home, etc. for the desired temperature to be attained. If the thermal capacity of the system were very small, the furnace capacity very large, and the heat losses very small, the error $(x_i - x_o)$ in the control system would be small. But, on the other hand, if the thermal capacity is large (a large home), the furnace capacity is small, and the outside temperature low, the deviations of the actual temperature from the desired temperature may be appreciable.

In principle the bang-bang control system differs little from the on-off control. But because it has the capability of providing both negative and positive control action it has more potential applications than the on-off controller. The bang-bang controller was one of the earliest types of servo system, because of its inherent simplicity, but, until comparatively recently, it has not been popular from a scientific point of view because, being non-linear in operation, it has proved difficult to analyse mathematically. However, during the past few years, there has been an upsurge of interest in bang-bang control systems because, for certain classes of control, they provide optimum performance. It is now possible, moreover, to analyse and to design scientifically bang-bang servos. The application of digital computers to the study of bang-bang servos has helped the design problem materially.

A typical bang-bang system is shown schematically in Fig. 30(a) and its basic control characteristic in Fig. 30(b). Depending on whether x_i is greater than, or less than x_o, the relay switches

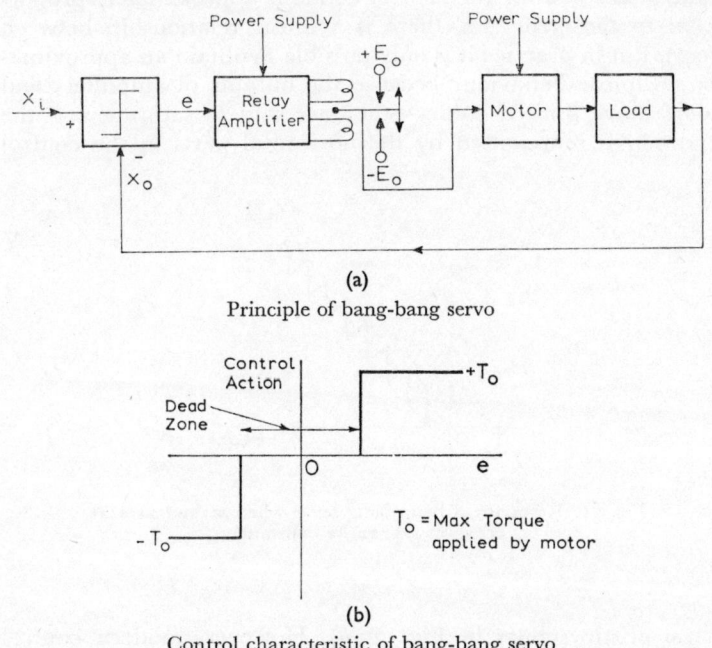

(a)
Principle of bang-bang servo

(b)
Control characteristic of bang-bang servo
Fig. 30.

positive or negative voltages respectively to the appropriate motor terminals. If, for example, the error signal is positive the motor will tend to drive the load in a positive direction. If, on the other hand, the error is negative the motor will apply maximum torque (T_o) in the negative direction. Control action is a function of the error. However, it depends only on the sign of the error. The behaviour of the output (x_o) for a continuously increasing value of x_i is shown in Fig. 31. In practice the "sharp corners" shown in the diagram are rounded off—nature objects to sudden changes as we have already seen in discussing the dynamic response of simple instruments, and tends to slow them down.

Let us return now to the continuous servo system shown in Fig. 28(a). It is usually referred to as a linear system because for small values of error the control action is approximately proportional to the error (i.e. there is a linear relationship between them). But in practice it is only possible to obtain an approximation to linear behaviour because the outputs of amplifiers and motors have limited values—they are said to saturate and the condition is represented by the horizontal parts in the control

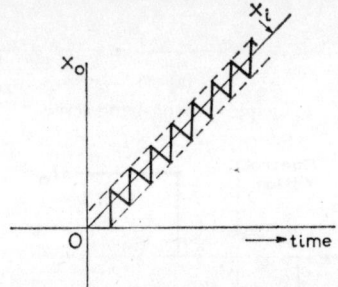

Fig. 31. Response of bang-bang servo when x_i increases at constant rate (x_i = constant)

characteristic shown in Fig. 27(b). However, modern control system theory and design not only takes such non-linearities into account but, in addition, studies how non-linear elements can be introduced into feedback control systems in order to improve performance. And this applies not only to the comparatively simple single variable control system of Fig. 27(a) but also to complex systems in which there may be several variables and several control loops. It is not surprising to learn that the introduction of nonlinear elements into control systems may improve their performance because the vast majority of biological servomechanisms are necessarily non-linear. This is an important point to bear in mind.

Static and Dynamic Behaviour

As in the example of the accelerometer, considered in the previous chapter, it is important to consider both the static and the dynamic accuracy of servos. If, for example, we suddenly apply a displacement to the input shaft of a servo the output shaft should align itself as quickly as possible with the new input shaft position. But if the load is massive, say a large radio telescope antenna, and if there is excessive friction in the bearings, the output member may not line up exactly with the input shaft and we say that a *static error* exists. (Note that in this example the bearing friction associated with the output shaft is static friction, or stiction, as opposed to viscous friction, dependent upon relative velocity, which we considered previously.)

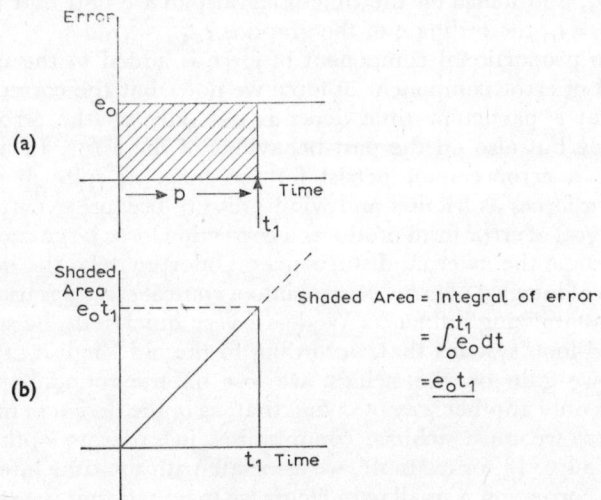

Fig. 32. Integral of error

In the state of equilibrium, or steady-state as we call it, the correcting force (or torque) exerted by the motor is equal and opposite to the stiction force. It is also proportional to the error. To reduce the error we can increase the amplification (or gain) of the system. For example, if $F =$ (force applied by the motor to move the load) $= Ke$, where K is the gain of the servo, and $e =$ error, obviously we must increase K. Unfortunately this is not always desirable as we shall see subsequently. Another method which is widely used is to introduce, in addition to a correcting force dependent on the error, an additional component of the correcting force which is equal to what is called the "time integral of the error". This is perhaps best explained by a diagram.

In Fig. 32(a) we assume that the error has a constant value e_o. If we determine the shaded area continually as a point p slides along the time axis, we can plot another graph shown in Fig. 32(b) in which this area (we call it the time integral of error (e)), is plotted against time. Thus, if the point p has reached time t_1 on the time scale the shaded area is clearly the product of e_o and t_1, and hence on the time-integral plot we find that at p, when $t = t_1$, the ordinate of the graph is $e_o t_1$.

If the proportional component of force is added to the time-integral of error component of force we note that the correcting action at a particular time depends not only on the error at that time but also on the past behaviour of the error. In other words, an error cannot persist for too long, in spite of such opposing forces as friction and wind pressure because eventually the integral of error term produces a correcting force large enough to overcome the external disturbances. Unfortunately, the introduction of integral of error control into a control system is usually an anti-stabilizing influence. We learn very quickly in the study of closed-loop systems that, according to the old English saying "what we gain on the swings, we lose on the roundabouts", which is only another way of saying that, as in the design of many processes, we must achieve compromises in order to optimize performance. If, for example, we associate with the time integral of error correction a small gain factor we may find that the stability of our system is not disturbed unduly. And, in combination with the stabilizing influence of "derivative of error" (introduced in Chapter 6), the introduction of integral of error control may be very beneficial.

Below, we try to summarize some of the problems which confront us when we set out to design a closed-loop control system. These are:

(a) The static error between input and output shafts must normally be as near zero as we can possibly make it.

(b) When the input shaft is rotating the dynamic error (or *tracking error* as it is sometimes called) between the input and the output shafts must be minimized. The major component of this error is usually due to viscous friction in the load system. For example, if, when the input and output shafts of a servo are both rotating with constant angular velocity, an angular error exists (i.e. the shafts are not in synchronism)—we call this error the velocity-lag. It is illustrated in Fig. 33. One of the ways to minimize the velocity-lag is by introducing a term in the control proportional to the time-integral of error. Thus, the time-integral of error component not only deals with static errors but also with dynamic errors.

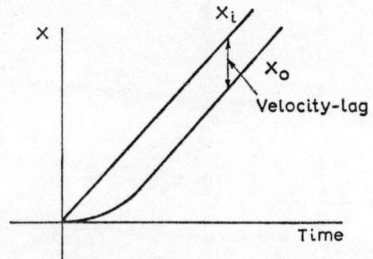

Fig. 33. Velocity-lag in servo behaviour

(c) A fundamental requirement in all servo systems is that they must be stable under all external conditions which are likely to arise. This means that if we apply a sudden change in the operating conditions, for example, a change of input, a change of wind velocity, a change in power level, or of the reference voltage, the servo system must eventually reach a steady-state, and in general it must reach this steady-state without undue oscillatory behaviour.

(d) The speed of response of a servo for a given load, normally expressed in terms of the time taken for the system to settle down after a sudden change of input, is another

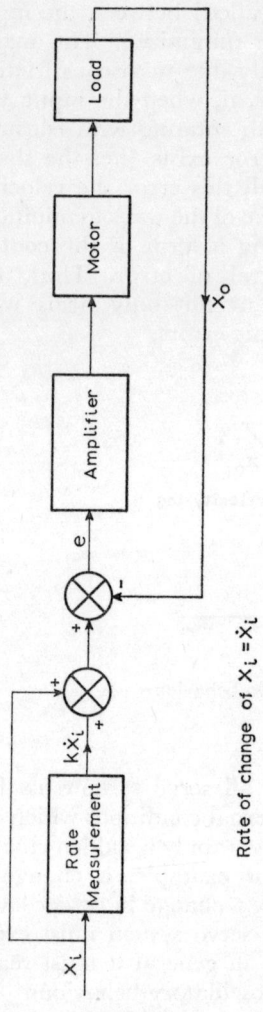

Servo system with velocity-lag compensation

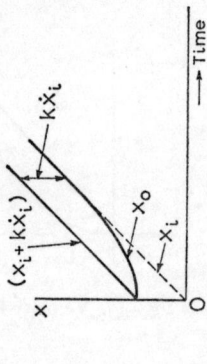

(b)

Response of servo with velocity-lag compensation

Fig. 34.

important parameter related to (c) above. High speed of response is often difficult to achieve because oscillatory behaviour is more likely to arise with "high-gain" systems.

In the design and manufacture of a product it is wise to seek out all relevant information relating to the product and to utilize the information optimally in the designing and manufacturing processes. This "principle", which we may call the "principle of optimum utilization of information", is particularly important in information feedback systems because the more information available, a priori, the less uncertainty there is in the operation of a system. For instance, in designing a simple servomechanism, if we know, from previous experience, that a dynamic lag proportional in magnitude to the input velocity will arise we should take this into account in designing the system. A method of approach which does not affect the stability of the system, because the closed cycle of operations is unaffected, is illustrated in Fig. 34(a). The idea is to anticipate the occurrence of the dynamic lag by adding a displacement to the input quantity which is proportional to the rate of change of the input quantity. We can then adjust the proportionality constant, say k as shown, so that we compensate for the inevitable dynamic lag by adding the anticipated lag to the input. The response of a simple servo system with velocity lag compensation is shown in Fig. 34(b).

Servomechanisms which include Human Operators

Although servo systems are normally regarded as automatic in operation many control systems incorporate human operators as key elements. Furthermore, when we pause to consider the large number of control operations in which human beings participate daily—driving a car is just one example—it is important to study the nature and behaviour of manual control systems. It is interesting to note, moreover, that a new engineering discipline, which involves the physiology and psychology of human beings, has been established within the past ten years or so—it is usually called "human factors engineering". Its importance cannot be over-emphasized because today, more than during any other period in history, man's machines constitute a highly significant part of his environment, and the relationship between man and machine calls for continual study.

During the last five years, for example, special attention has been paid, by scientists and engineers, to such human factors problems, chosen at random, as,

(a) the design of "safe" automobiles,
(b) the physiological, psychological, and physical characteristics required in manned space flights—it is important to know the astronaut's characteristics as a flight controller and how he will react under various flight conditions such as lift-off, capsule instability, vehicle re-entry, etc.,
(c) the reasons why industrial accidents occur especially when machines are involved,
(d) the improvement of man-machine languages used, for example, when man communicates with a computer.

Each of these problems involved information feedback, although some of them fall outside the scope of this book. However, a basic understanding of the nature of manual control systems is obviously sufficiently important to justify a brief treatment.

Figure 35 shows the main components of a simple manual control system. The broken lines indicate internal feedback channels in the human central nervous system. Needless to say Fig. 35 is a considerably over-simplified portrayal of the true situation since probably several hundreds, or even thousands, of feedback channels would be operative in the operator's body during the performance of the control task.

The display unit might be a cathode ray tube, an instrument dial, the field of a telescope, or perhaps even the "feel" of a system (for example, we control many processes using multi-sensory perception—riding a bicycle, and driving a car are good examples). The operator's sensors, usually his eyes, since the display is frequently visual, provide the primary information. But past experience, combined with logical ability, also help the operator to determine the appropriate corrective action to take. In the example shown in Fig. 36 it is assumed that the operator actuates the control by means of a joystick or handwheel. Having taken the decision to move the joystick in one way or another, the operator's brain signals the muscles of his arms, and hands, and a force is applied to the joystick. But the application of this

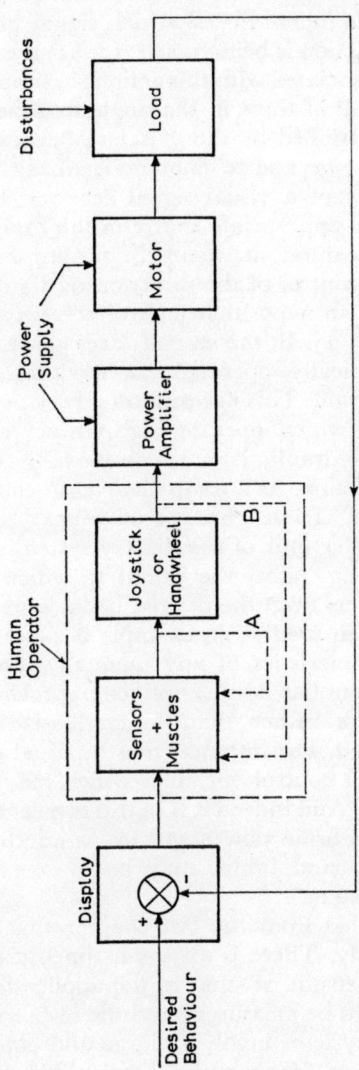

Fig. 35. A manual control system

force immediately triggers off stretch receptors and information feedback channels (nerve fibres) which signal back to the brain that the desired action is being taken. In fact there may be many feedback paths associated with this action; to simplify the diagram I have included all of these in the single feedback path denoted by A. The force applied by the muscles of arm and hand move the joystick and give rise to another feedback path, B, which consists essentially of a visual signal received by the eye and transmitted to the appropriate centre in the brain.

The joystick position, in many important systems such as, for example, the control of the direction of flight of an aircraft, acts as the input to a position control servo system similar to that shown in Fig. 25. In the case of large airliners this servo is normally hydraulically operated, rather than electrically as shown in the diagram. This necessitates power being supplied by hydraulic pumps which operate high-power relays, which in turn actuate the hydraulic jacks which move the control surfaces in the desired direction. As a result changes in course or height of the aircraft occur. These changes of course, or altitude, are reflected in the behaviour of the display system which indicates to the operator (e.g. pilot) the extent to which the behaviour of the aircraft differs from the desired behaviour. The control of an aircraft has been used as an example because it incorporates most of the characteristics of any manually controlled system. However, the system has been simplified appreciably in order to illustrate principles rather than to emphasize details of the technology involved. For instance, most manual control systems incorporate several control variables which may be interacting one with the other. And indeed it is in this respect that the human operator, using his brain power and his wonderful coordination of muscles, nerves and limbs, may be more effective than a fully automatic system.

It will be recalled from the last chapter that no instrument acts instantaneously. There is always a time-delay between the excitation of an instrument (that is, the application of the input quantity which is to be measured) and the response of the instrument. In control systems involving large and complex processes and machines such as, for example, chemical plants, the economic activity of a nation, large airliners, etc. there may be large exponential time-constants involved ranging in magnitude from several seconds to several hours, and perhaps even to several days or months. As we shall see in Chapter 6 the effect of these time-delays may be to cause oscillatory behaviour of the system and perhaps instability.

The pilot of a large airliner, or for that matter the driver of an automobile, has to take into account the total effect of a large number of time-delays and he has to predict ahead far enough to make intelligent decisions. His task is all the more difficult when external disturbances such as turbulent air affect his multi-loop control system. The pilot correlates an awesome array of visual, auditory and tactile data sources which involve a fantastic number of feedback channels. Similarly, but at a lower level, the automobile driver receives continually a large quantity of information which must be coordinated and upon which his decisions are continually made. Driving could not

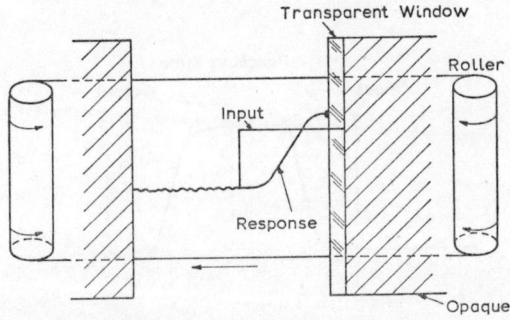

Fig. 36. Determination of response of human operator to a step function

readily be mechanized. In view of the complexity of the task it behoves us, at all times when driving, to be as alert as possible in order to recognize change with minimum delay.

I mentioned, at the beginning of this chapter, that one of the disadvantages of human operators in the control of processes is the inherent time-lag between stimulation and response which is characteristic of all human beings. But in systems where the over-all time delays are measured in tens of seconds, minutes, hours, etc. the effect of human reaction time may not be significant. This may be the case in such tasks as piloting an aircraft because the delays between, for instance, the time a control surface is moved and the time the aircraft achieves a new course may be several seconds while the average value of human reaction time is in the order of 0·3 seconds.

But it is nevertheless important to know how a human operator behaves when subjected to a sensory stimulus so that we will be in a better position to design man-machine systems, such as automobiles, on a scientific basis. In complex systems, such as the control of aircraft, so many feedback loops are involved, a few of the basic loops are shown in Fig. 35, that it is possible for internal defects to cause malfunction in the system and in such cases it is highly important that the pilot, or flight engineer, should detect the change and take the necessary action as rapidly as possible. For such reasons it is important to study the response of human operators in much the same way as we study the response of instruments and of servo systems.

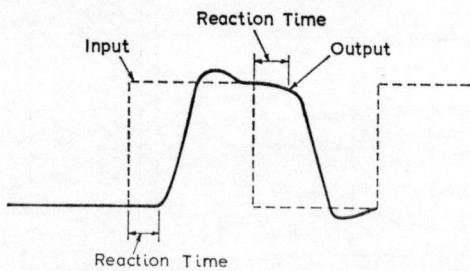

Fig. 37. Response of human operator to a square function

A simple apparatus for such a study is shown in Fig. 36. A roll of paper, upon which a series of input step functions are drawn at random intervals, can be moved at speeds of, say, 1 to 3 inches a second in the direction shown. A human operator is required to "track", using a pencil, the input by trying to keep the point of his pencil at all times on the pre-drawn line. Obviously it is impossible to do this accurately when a step occurs and the sort of response we obtain is shown in Fig. 37. If no advance information is available concerning the imminent arrival of the input step function we obtain a true reaction time response. If, on the other hand, a transparent window is provided, as shown in the diagram, giving the subject some indication of what is coming, his tracking accuracy will improve. In general, the accuracy of tracking will increase as the width of the window is increased and as we decrease the linear speed of the paper. This fairly obvious conclusion exemplifies the importance of anticipation in control situations.

Figure 37 defines the reaction time as the time interval between the incidence of the input signal and the instant when response to the stimulation begins. Physiologically, we can regard the reaction time as consisting of two components, one component is the time taken for the stimulation signal to be transmitted, via nerve fibres, to the brain and to be accommodated and the second component is the time taken for the action signal to be transmitted from the brain to excite the appropriate muscles and to initiate action. The response curve, shown in the diagram, comprises the finite time delay which we have called reaction time, and a response function which normally includes a single overshoot. It will be noted that the nature of the total response curve differs appreciably from that which would be obtained using a simple instrument involving a single exponential delay. The delays which characterize the human operator are undesirable when high-speed response is a requirement. But when judgement is required, and concepts must be formed, in order to optimize the operation of a complex control system, the human operator is often the most superlative control element available.

Some Wartime Developments

From time to time in this book I have mentioned the important research in the field of information feedback control systems which was carried out during World War II. I pointed out, for example, that cybernetic science was founded largely as a result of work in the field of anti-aircraft defence. In retrospect, perhaps the main contributions of World War II technology to control science and engineering were essentially four-fold, namely:

(a) The development of electrical and hydraulic servomechanisms, within the power range 50 watts to 500 kilowatts, the former for automatic analogue computers and for the control of small radar "dishes" of perhaps 50 centimetres diameter, and the latter for the control of heavy naval armament, laid the foundations for the multiplicity of uses which have been found for servo-mechanisms in peace-time industry.

(b) For the first time, on a large scale, scientists and engineers came up against the problem of achieving precision control when the input data was very impure, e.g. "noisy". With the early radar equipment, for example, the key problem was to separate the real from the spurious data. Mathematicians, scientists and engineers came up with many ingenious data filtering systems and considerable success was achieved. So much so that, by 1945, auto-tracking radars with average tracking errors less than $\frac{1}{4}°$ were available. Similar problems arise in the control of nuclear power reactors, in tracking satellites with radio telescopes, in the control of chemical plants, etc. and the same basic design techniques, which were evolved during World War II, still apply.

(c) The advent of the systemic approach to the optimization of complex systems undoubtedly arose as a result of the urgent need to synthesize servomechanisms from standard building blocks. This subject was introduced in Chapter 2. It deserves mentioning again because of its importance in the present-day framework of technological and managerial evolution.

(d) The first fundamental studies of man-machine systems were carried out in connection with the manual control of the early radar equipment and the mechanical analogue computers (e.g. anti-aircraft predictors). As was pointed out previously, radar information requires filtering and the early radar operators had considerable difficulty in maintaining smooth tracking-rates. Further, unsmoothed radar information when fed into a predictor caused erratic performance, and it soon became clear that detailed studies of the effectiveness of human operators as radar operators was essential. The early studies blossomed into comprehensive research programmes, which, during the past twenty years have given rise to "human factors engineering".

5. Models

One of man's innate characteristics is his urge to mimic and analogize. Its social manifestation has been the evolution of the performing arts through the creation of drama, satire, and the theatre. Similarly, and also of great social and literary significance, is the metaphor—"to be the master of metaphor is the greatest poetic gift . . . metaphor is formed on the basis of analogy" writes Aristotle in his "Poetics". Metaphor in science is synonymous with the physical and mathematical model.

An associated human characteristic is man's desire to create artefacts with characteristics similar to his own. The words "like" and "likeness" have much deeper significance than might appear at first sight because a major component of our thought processes is probably concerned with determining the degree of likeness between writings, or objects, or systems, or situations, or philosophies. The fine arts, especially sculpture and painting, exemplify man's urge to create likenesses in his own image and the image of his environment, and some branches of technology fall into the same category. For example, the early automata, particularly the mechanical figures which strike the hour bells of some mediaeval clocks, are excellent examples. The reader may well ask—what has this to do with cybernetics and the feedback principle? This is a good question which this chapter attempts to answer.

During the past twenty years or so the art of modelling and simulating systems has established itself as one of the most important research and design techniques available to science and engineering. This is not surprising because many of us believe that man searches continually for likenesses, in order to learn about his environment, by evolving patterns and structures in knowledge. For many years scientists have been conscious of the importance of models in scientific research and some scientists regard science itself as necessarily a model of reality in much the same way as the theatre is a model of society. The great physicist Clerk Maxwell once stated that purely mathematical expressions are not readily understandable without physical models.

In the physical and biological sciences models can often be regarded as hypotheses that provide the starting point for specific scientific researches. The process of developing a theory in the physical sciences, in the sense of hypothesis building, is admirably illustrated in Fig. 38. Here we see how mathematics and physics interact. After specifying a *real problem* (e.g. the effect of a magnetic

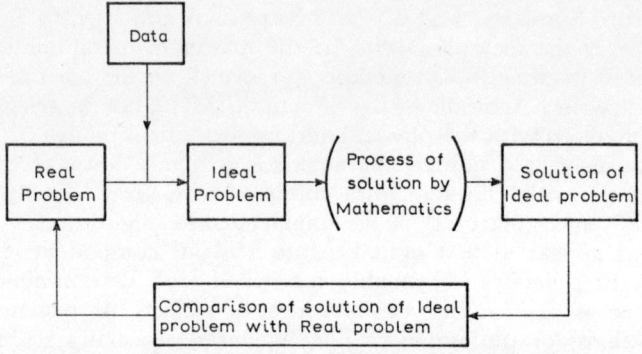

Fig. 38. Schematic representation of the mathematical solution of a problem in physics. (Adapted from Fig. 2 of Sir Graham Sutton's book *Mathematics in Action*. Reproduced by permission of G. Bell & Sons Ltd.)

field on a current carrying conductor) the physicist collects all appropriate data relating to the problem (e.g. the magnetic field intensity and the magnitude and direction of the current) and he develops an idealized mathematical description of the real system. In the cases of complex problems this may be a very time-consuming task. The solution of the *ideal problem* by mathematics is then carried out and the results obtained are compared with experimental results. If agreement exists between the two sets of results we consider the theory to be verified. The hypothesis building process shown in Fig. 38 is closely related to the process of mathematical model building.

Models, such as that of Bohr of the atom, gave scientists insight into atomic structure, and provided the basis for modern atomic physics and chemistry, and it helped, perhaps more than any other single advance, scientists to understand the nature of matter. More recently the model of the structure of the DNA molecule, and its interpretation due to Watson and Crick, has shed great light on the fundamental processes of biology.

The models I will introduce will be both physical and mathematical. Perhaps the idea of a mathematical model will be new but, as we will see, it is not difficult to understand.* Whenever we can describe natural phenomena, or man-made systems, in terms of mathematical equations we say that we have developed a mathematical model of the system. The system can then be studied by either solving the mathematical equations using pencil and paper or, when the amount of numerical computation required is excessive, by using a general-purpose digital computer. Such models are abstract in the sense that they may not conjure up visions of the system under study, but they nevertheless describe the responses of the real system when it is subjected to various inputs and changes. Furthermore, it is important to note that models only provide approximations to system behaviour, and mathematical models, in particular, are essentially idealizations of the systems they represent, e.g. in mechanical systems friction is often ignored, and in electrical systems ideal resistors, capacitors, etc. are assumed.

The beauty of the model approach to the study of physical systems, or to engineering design, lies in its flexibility. Models vary considerably in their degree of complexity and it is worthwhile noting that the models of the physical sciences, such as those of the atom, the solar system, wave motion, and many others are comparatively simple compared with many engineering design models, and with the models which have been developed in the biological sciences and the social sciences. Once we have determined the nature of a model, physical or mathematical, it can be used for experiments. For example, we may wish to predict the behaviour of the real system when subjected to a variety of internal and/or external changes. These changes can be simulated approximately by the model and detailed studies carried out. Of course, in the cases of many systems, experimentation

* See, for example, "Mathematics in Action". O. G. Sutton; G. Bell & Sons Ltd., London and Harper Brothers, New York, for a survey of some of the many elegant mathematical models used in the physical sciences.

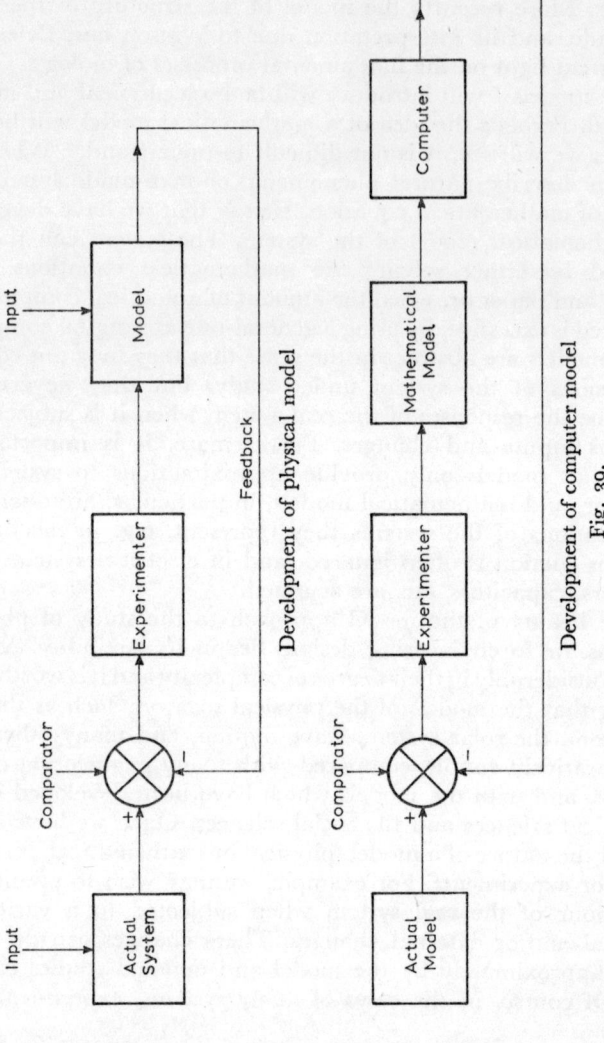

Development of physical model

Development of computer model

Fig. 39.

with the system itself might be out of the question because of danger to life and limb, or perhaps because of the high costs involved.

Let us consider first the process of developing a model. It is of particular interest because of its necessarily closed-loop character as demonstrated in Figs. 39(a) and (b).

In Fig. 39(a) it is assumed that the system under study exists, and that in order to determine its behaviour when subjected to unusual conditions we are in the process of building a model. The behaviour of the system and its model, under normal conditions, are compared and the experimenter modifies the parameters of the model until its behaviour coincides approximately with that of the system. The diagram illustrates how information feedback is involved. The model itself can now be used to study the special conditions in which the experimenter is interested. By measuring the model's performance he obtains an approximation to the behaviour of the real system under similar conditions.

Figure 39(b), which is, of course, purely schematic, shows ideally how the mathematical model of a complex system might be obtained. It shows how the model is developed by comparing the system behaviour with the corresponding computer solutions. The experimenter changes the mathematical model until an adequate degree of correspondence between the computer output and the system response results. Such procedures usually require considerable mathematical ability and ingenuity especially in the study of systems which involve many variables and where the relations between them are complex. And it is important to note that all models are, at best, approximations and special care is required to ascertain the degree of equivalence between system and model. But because the sole purpose of a model is to predict system behaviour, it usually happens that a reasonable approximation is all that is required. The more accurate the model the more accurate the prediction.

Alternatively, if we are concerned with building, rather than analysing, a system the design can often be appreciably facilitated by using model investigations. For instance, a basic attribute of many models is due to the speeding up of the time-scale of operation. This means that model experiments can be carried out in a fraction of the time required to carry out the equivalent experiments using the actual system. And as a result it is possible to explore most foreseeable conditions. In practice, for example, space vehicles, supersonic aircraft, and nuclear reactors are designed on the basis of comprehensive computer simulation studies which may simulate several hours or days of actual operation in perhaps a few minutes. However, all possibilities are rarely foreseen during simulator studies, and many examples of unpredictable problems have been reported in, for example, space missions when the human factor has frequently had to make up for deficiencies in the operation of mechanical and electronic systems.

In addition to space and other aerodynamic models (e.g. the study of aerodynamic behaviour using models mounted in wind tunnels), and nuclear reactors, dynamic models have been used widely to study the silting of river estuaries, to simulate the behaviour of chemical plants, to study economic systems, and, quite recently, to study simple biological systems. While the computer simulations of production processes, road traffic flow in cities, air and rail transportation systems, and electric power generating and distribution systems, and many others are becoming well recognized techniques.

An important attribute of the model arises from the fact that some models have universal applicability. For instance, a mathematical model of wave motion can be used in the study of acoustics, wave-guides used in radar equipment, ocean waves, and, with some modifications, in the determination of atomic structure (i.e. by applying the concepts of wave mechanics). Some mathematical models of well-known physical phenomena are outlined below.

Mathematical Models

As a first example consider the mathematical model which applies to all physical situations in which one variable is related linearly to another variable. For example, when we heat a metal rod the linear expansion of the rod is proportional to the increase in temperature. Similarly, the distance travelled by an object moving with constant velocity is proportional to the time of travel, the extension of a linear spring depends linearly on the magnitude of the force applied at one end of the spring, the height of a liquid in a cylindrical tank depends linearly on the rate of flow of liquid into the tank, and so on.

MODELS

The mathematical model which applies to all these situations can be written in the form,

$$y = ax + b$$

in which a and b are constants.

If this equation relates to the thermal expansion of a metal rod the variables y and x would correspond, respectively, to the length of the rod when the temperature is $x°$, and the temperature $x°$. The constants a and b would be, respectively, the product of the coefficient of linear expansion of the metal multiplied by the length at $0°$, and the length of the bar when the temperature is $0°$. When plotted in the form of a graph the result is as shown in Fig. 40. Using the graph, or the simple algebraic relationship

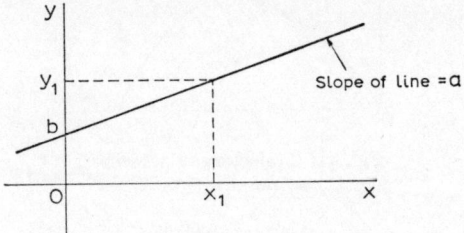

Fig. 40. Graph of $y = ax + b$

between x and y given above, we can predict the length of the metal rod for a wide range of temperatures (lower, of course, than the melting point temperature of the metal!) without actually measuring the length of the bar at these temperatures. This elementary mathematical model illustrates a basic property of all models—they can be used for prediction purposes. Furthermore, all physical, biological, economic, etc. processes which can be described by the linear algebraic relationship given in the above equation are representable by the same model. Such an example is, of course, trivial and it would be unnecessary to build a physical model because, given the values of x, a, and b, the determination of the corresponding value of y is easy. But many scientific and engineering problems involve complicated mathematical models and in these cases it may be necessary to solve the corresponding mathematical equations by means of a computer—the more physical systems that can be represented by a single mathematical model, in general, the more powerful the model.

The idea of the mathematical model is so important in the world of science that three more examples, taken from different scientific fields, are presented below. Two of the models introduce mathematics which may be unfamiliar to the reader but, since I am merely trying to illustrate a principle, only superficial understanding of the mathematical symbolism is necessary.

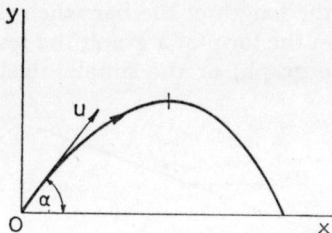

Fig. 41. Trajectory of a baseball

If we neglect air resistance and assume that the acceleration due to gravity "g" is constant, the trajectory of a baseball, or a shell, is shown in Fig. 41. It is assumed that the initial velocity of the baseball is u (feet/second) and that the initial direction of the trajectory makes an angle α with the horizontal direction. The equations of motion of the baseball can be readily obtained by applying Newton's Laws of Motion. They can be written,

$$x = u \cdot t \cdot \cos \alpha,$$

$$y = u \cdot t \cdot \sin \alpha + \tfrac{1}{2}gt^2.$$

These equations give the (x, y) coordinates of the baseball, or shell, for any given time t seconds—assume that at the instant the ball is thrown $t = 0$. The equations define a mathematical model of the system assuming the values of x, y, and α are given at $t = 0$, but of course it is the model appropriate to a vacuum for in reality air resistance is very important for both shells and baseballs.

I referred previously to an important physical law which we call the Law of Exponential Decay. This law applies to a wide range of physical phenomena. It applies, for example, to the level of radio-activity of a radio-active source which has been active for a given time, to the temperature of liquid in a container which has been cooling for a given time, and to the height of liquid in a tank which has been discharging liquid through a valve for a given time, and so on. The law applies to all systems and processes in which the rate of change of a variable, say y, depends on the value of y itself. The relationship can be written,

$$\text{rate of change of } y = \frac{dy}{dt} = \dot{y} = -\frac{y}{T}$$

in which T is the time-constant of decay of the system.* (The minus sign is introduced to account for the fact that the system is decaying in the sense that the temperature of the liquid, for example, is falling.)

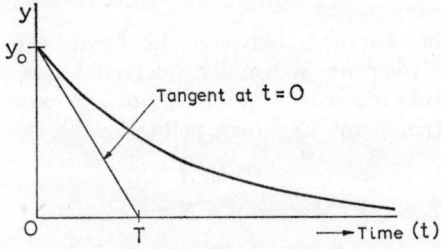

Fig. 42. Law of exponential decay

Figure 42, in which y_0 is the value of y at time zero, shows a typical exponentially decaying function. The appropriate mathematical model, written above in the form of a first-order differential equation, has wide application. It will be noted that the model is closely related to that describing the dynamic behaviour of a simple instrument.

* Later in this chapter the relationship is given in an alternate form.

Consider now a model of a different kind. It introduces the important mathematical entity which we call a "matrix". It has great significance in a wide range of physical problems including atomic physics. I will illustrate it by what has come to be known as "The Travelling Salesman" problem. It is an important problem in operations research.

Suppose a travelling salesman has to visit several towns which we will call towns 1, 2, 3, 4, etc. and that he wishes to select a route, perhaps starting at town 1, which minimizes the total distance he has to travel.

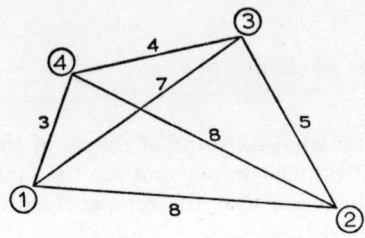

Fig. 43. A network of towns

Suppose the distances between the towns are as shown in Fig. 43. The diagram is usually referred to as a "network". The information given in Fig. 43 can also be expressed symbolically in "matrix form" as shown below:

Table 1

(Matrix of a Network)

Town	1	2	3	4
1	0	8	7	3
2	8	0	5	8
3	7	5	0	4
4	3	8	4	0

If we scan across row 2, for example, we note that the distance between town 2 and town 1 is 8 miles, the distance between town 2 and town 2 is zero, the distance between town 2 and town 3 is 5 miles, etc. It will be seen that the diagonal elements of the matrix are all zero and that the matrix is symmetrical about the

MODELS

diagonal—one side is the "mirror" image of the other. The symmetrical characteristic arises, of course, because the distance between towns 1 and 4, say, is the same as the distance between towns 4 and 1. The matrix may be regarded as a model of the road network joining the towns.

The formulation of network problems of this kind in terms of matrix notation lends itself to the elegant and powerful methods of matrix algebra as well as to computer methods of solution. If, in the previous problem, there were 50 towns (or warehouses, or plants, or components, etc.) instead of only four, the problem of determining the best route becomes extremely complicated.

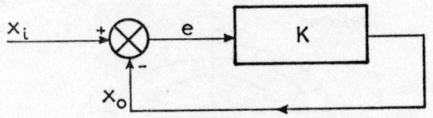

Fig. 44. Idealised single-loop control system

The reason is that whereas for the 4-town network the number of alternative routes, assuming we always start, say from town 1, is only six, the number of alternatives for a 50-town network is a fantastically large number. Fortunately, computer methods of handling large networks are available.

As a final example of a mathematical model consider the idealized single-loop automatic control system shown in block diagram form in Fig. 44. The system is idealized because it is assumed that no time delays exist and the operation of the control is assumed to be instantaneous. The equations describing the behaviour of the system, which can be regarded as a mathematical model of the system, are:

$$e = x_i - x_o$$
$$x_o = Ke$$

which reduce to the single equation,

$$x_o = \frac{Kx_i}{1 + K}$$

When K is large (compared with unity) the value of x_o approaches that of x_i.

Physical Models

The mathematical models we have been talking about may be studied and used in two ways. First, especially in the cases of elementary mathematical models, the equations of the mathematical model can be solved, by standard mathematical techniques, for all the situations in which we are interested. For instance, if the mathematical model turns out to be an algebraic quadratic equation, as in the case of the baseball trajectory model, we can readily solve the equation for given values of the initial

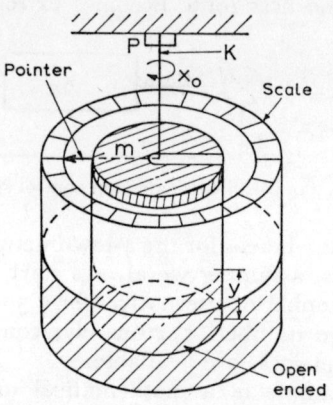

Fig. 45. Model for studying oscillatory behaviour

velocity and for given initial angles of the trajectory. Second, if the mathematical model is complex and does not lend itself to mathematical methods of solution, we solve the equations, which may involve matrices, and/or differential coefficients (as defined in the differential calculus) by computer methods.

Computers may be *analogue*, *digital* or *hybrid*. As the name implies analogue computers operate in terms of physical analogues. In a slide rule, for example, a number is represented by a length. In electronic analogue computers, such as those used aboard some space vehicles (on account of their inherent simplicity), numbers are represented by voltages. In digital computers, on the other hand, numbers may be represented in a variety of ways, including the states of counters. Theoretically, a digital computer can be built with unlimited accuracy, in contrast with an analogue computer whose accuracy is determined by the accuracy with which we can measure length, voltage, etc.

It is sometimes useful to study the dynamic behaviour of physical systems by means of special-purpose models. A typical, albeit simple, model is shown in Fig. 45. It consists essentially of a torsion pendulum in which the mass suspended by the suspension wire is an inverted cylindrical can upon which cylindrical weights can be placed as shown. The system may be used to study the damping effects of various kinds of liquid such as might be used, for example, in the shock absorbers of automobiles or aircraft landing gear. If the fluid has a low coefficient of viscosity the damping effect is small. If the liquid has a high coefficient of viscosity the damping effect is large. Note, also, that the damping torque is proportional to the length of the cylindrical can immersed in the liquid.

One series of experiments, using this simple model, can be performed by displacing the can from its equilibrium position through an angle of about 45° and subsequently, by means of stop-watch and a fixed scale, determining approximately the behaviour of the can. Typical responses of the system are similar to those shown in Fig. 46. If the liquid is "Newtonian", that is, the viscous friction torque acting on the walls of the cylinder is proportional to the angular velocity of the cylinder, we can readily establish a mathematical model of this system and solve it by well-known methods. (As a matter of fact, the mathematical model of the torsion pendulum model is identical in form with the mathematical model of the accelerometer we considered in Chapter 3.) If the damping liquid is non-Newtonian, the model can be used to study the behaviour of a class of non-linearly damped systems which are not readily amenable to mathematical solution.

The physical model shown in Fig. 45 has many uses. It is not difficult to show, for example, that the dynamic behaviour of the system corresponds closely with the dynamic behaviour of simple servomechanisms, and with the dynamic behaviour of a wide range of measuring instruments. As a piece of laboratory apparatus for studying oscillatory motion it is strongly recommended.

The torsion pendulum can be regarded as a special purpose physical model. Its usefulness as a model is enhanced because its parameters are readily variable, and it can be used to study both linear and non-linear (e.g. non-linear damping and non-linear spring) systems. For instance, we can increase the spring stiffness (K) of the system by decreasing the length of the suspension and vice versa. If K is increased by a factor of 2, the natural frequency of oscillation of the pendulum is increased by a factor of $\sqrt{2}$. Similarly, the suspended mass m may be changed by adding or subtracting weights—if we change m, say, to $2m$, the natural frequency of the oscillatory motion, when the system is undamped, is reduced by a factor of $\sqrt{2}$. Furthermore, the damping coefficient which characterizes the system can be modified by raising or lowering the level of the damping liquid

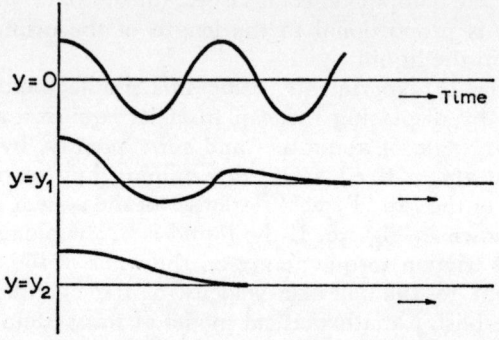

Fig. 46. Responses of torsion pendulum for increasing depths of immersion of can in damping fluid

in the tank. And, in addition, the damping liquid can easily be replaced when desired and the model can be used, as mentioned previously, for experimentally determining the viscous damping characteristics of various liquids, including non-Newtonian liquids.

Of more general applicability, however, as a model or simulator is the electronic analogue computer which can be programmed to study systems whose mathematical models are in the form of differential equations or sets of differential equations. The standard electronic analogue computer incorporates components which are capable of carrying out addition, multiplication, integration (e.g. determination of area under a graph), the generation of mathematical functions like x^2, sine x, log x, and many others. There have been widespread applications of electronic computers to studies in the field of aircraft design, the guidance of unmanned space vehicles, simulation of chemical plants, the stability of electrical power transmission and distribution systems, and a variety of others.

As a first step in setting-up, or programming, an analogue or a digital computer it is frequently useful to obtain a diagrammatic representation of the system under study illustrating the relationships and interdependence of key system variables. Such diagrams are often called information flow diagrams and many forms are in current use. The familiar digital computer flow diagrams, used widely in the programming of computers, are a special class of information flow diagram. Another class which is proving valuable in design and research problems in various scientific and engineering fields is the so-called *signal flowgraph*. The method, which was developed independently by Mason at M.I.T. and Tustin in England, is considered below in some detail.

The Signal Flowgraph

Familiarity with the basic ideas of signal flowgraphs is desirable for several reasons which will emerge later. But perhaps the most important reason is the degree of insight into system behaviour, far exceeding that obtained by mere algebraic manipulations, which they provide. Further, and the reason for introducing them in this chapter, signal flowgraphs may be regarded as dynamic models of systems. Their full potential in this latter respect has only recently been recognized.

Signal flowgraphs form an integral part of a new branch of applied mathematics which has been called "graph theory". However, it is not my object to present, even if I were in a position to do so, the theory of signal flowgraphs but rather to introduce them as an aid to understanding the nature of certain physical, biological, economic, etc. systems.

The signal flowgraph was developed in the first place to illustrate diagrammatically how the key variables of a system are interrelated. In many physical and chemical systems, for example, the interactions between key quantities such as temperature, pressure, volume, etc. may be obscure, and in such systems the signal flowgraph frequently helps us to obtain a qualitative appreciation of what is going on. And of increasing importance is the use of signal flowgraphs as the first step in the programming of a numerical computation or in programming a computer.

A flowgraph is essentially a diagrammatic portrayal of a mathematical model. It represents a system of equations. It is comprised of a set of "nodes", symbolized by small circles, each of which represents a variable, a parameter, a coefficient, or a constant of the system under consideration. When a relationship exists between one "node" and another, it is represented by a "directed branch"—this is merely a line, joining the two nodes,

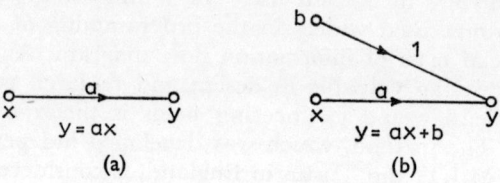

Fig. 47. Elementary flowgraphs

which is characterized by an arrow showing the direction of the dependence and the appropriate mathematical operation which expresses the relationship. We will soon discover, by considering a few examples, that a variety of configurations may arise, including closed-loops and self-loops. All this sounds complicated but the following examples of flowgraphs, which represent certain physical phenomena, will help to clarify the situation.

Consider first the flowgraph of the general linear system described by the mathematical equation (or model)

$$y = ax + b.$$

It has already been shown that this model describes an important class of physical processes such as, for example, the thermal expansion of a metal bar. We assume that the constant coefficients a and b, and the independent variable x (in the model of the linear thermal expansion of a bar, x is the temperature of the bar) are given, and y, the dependent variable, is required. First we let $b = 0$ and show how to represent the relationship between y and x. The corresponding flowgraph consisting of two "nodes" and a single branch joining them is shown in Fig. 47(a). In the general case when $b \neq 0$, the flowgraph for the

MODELS

linear model is modified as shown in Fig. 47(b). The arrows on the branches $x \rightarrow y$ and $b \rightarrow y$ are directed "into y", in other words to determine y we must know x and a and b. No feedback branch is involved in this flowgraph because the value of y is determined solely from data which is independent of y. The flowgraphs of Fig. 47 are called open-loop or open-sequence graphs.

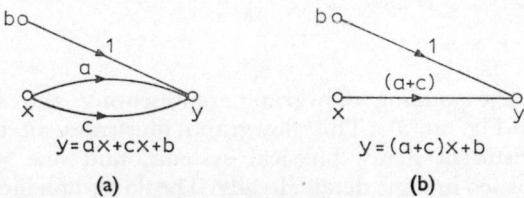

Fig. 48. Demonstrating replacement of two parallel branches by a single branch

If the linear relationship takes the form,

$$y = ax + cx + b,$$

the modified flowgraph is shown in Fig. 48(a). But this relationship can also be written in the form,

$$y = (a + c)x + b,$$

and the corresponding flowgraph is shown in Fig. 48(b). The two flowgraphs are, of course, identical and demonstrate how parallel branches joining two nodes can be reduced to a single branch. Similarly, if

$$y = ax \quad \text{and} \quad z = by,$$

we deduce directly that $z = abx$, and in terms of the corresponding flowgraph representation we can reduce a flowgraph involving three nodes and two branches to a flowgraph involving two nodes and a single branch connecting them. Several other methods of reducing flowgraphs have been devised and have proved to be extremely useful in the "reduction" of complex systems.

Let us consider now an example of a flowgraph involving several variables. Let the mathematical model of a physical (or biological, or economic) system be defined by the following set of simultaneous equations:

$$x_2 = ax_1 - x_5$$
$$x_3 = bx_2$$
$$x_4 = cx_3$$
$$x_5 = dx_4$$

The corresponding flowgraph representing the system is shown in Fig. 49(a). This flowgraph illustrates an important characteristic of many physical systems, and one which we have discussed in some detail already. The flowgraph incorporates a negative feedback branch, which interconnects the variables x_5 and x_2, and which is negative because of the (-1) weighting factor. If we consider the flowgraph as a representation of how one variable depends on other variables (this is one of the flowgraph's major attributes), we note that since the feedback branch in Fig. 49(a) can be thought of as "feeding back" information from a later to an earlier point in the cascade of branches which terminates in x_5 then clearly the value of the variable x_5 depends upon itself. All this means algebraically is that if we assume x_1 is given, the mathematical model defined above can be reduced, algebraically, to the relationship

$$x_5 = bcd(ax_1 - x_5).$$

And the corresponding flowgraph for this relationship is shown in Fig. 49(b). An alternative configuration is shown in Fig. 49(c). This third flowgraph, which is readily shown to be equivalent to the other two, includes a so-called "self-loop". It illustrates in a highly pictorial way that x_5 actually does depend upon its own behaviour. The next example deals with a physical situation which exemplifies flowgraphs of this kind. Indeed, all systems which involve physical or intrinsic feedback loops can be reduced to flowgraphs which involve branches and self-loops.

We will consider a system which exemplifies the law of exponential decay. Out of the many possible physical phenomena which might have been chosen I have picked a comparatively simple hydraulic system. It is shown diagrammatically in Fig. 50(a). It consists essentially of a cylindrical tank containing liquid, and an outflow controlled by a valve. This simple model can be multiplicated, for example, for the study of cascaded reservoirs, and it has proved invaluable in such studies.

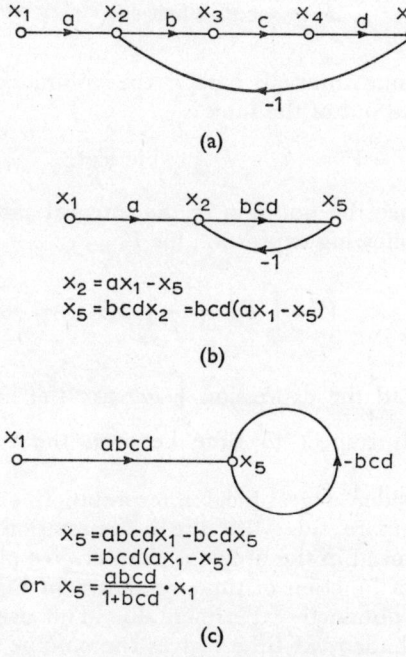

Fig. 49. An equivalent set of flowgraphs characterised by negative feedback

With a fixed setting of the valve, which we assume gives a "stream-lined" outflow, we see intuitively that the rate of the outflow depends only on the height of liquid in the tank. If the tank is full the rate of outflow is appeciably greater than if it is nearly empty. In fact the rate of out-flow (i.e. the outflow per second) is proportional to the height of liquid in the tank; it is also proportional to the valve opening.

Let h_o be the height of liquid in the tank at $t = 0$, the instant at which the valve is opened to a pre-determined setting, and let A be the cross-sectional area of the tank, and r the "resistance" of the valve and outflow tube. If h is the height of liquid at time t, then for a given valve setting r, the outflow rate F is given by,

$$F = \frac{h}{r} \text{ cubic feet/sec.}$$

During the time interval, 0 to t, the volume of liquid (V) which has flowed out of the tank is,

$$V = (h_o - h)A \text{ cubic feet.}$$

If we introduce the notation of the integral calculus we can also write the following expression for V,

$$V = \int_0^t F dt = \frac{1}{r} \int_0^t h dt$$

in which we read the expression $\int_0^t F dt$ as "the integral of the variable F with respect to time between the range of time $t = 0$ to t sec."

We will consider a graphical interpretation of the integral expression—compare this with the interpretation of "integral of error" introduced in the previous chapter. We plot the output flow rate F, as a function of time, as shown in Fig. 50(b)—this graph can be obtained experimentally. The area under the curve (shown shaded) at time t gives the volume (V) of liquid which has flowed out of the tank. We might measure it experimentally using a second tank. The process of integration is, in the present context, merely an area-finding operation.

But the area under the curve, for the time period $t = 0$ to t, can also be equated to $A(h_o - h)$ which is, of course, V. Fig. 50(c) shows the graph of $A(h_o - h)$ plotted against t—its ordinate at time t gives the magnitude of the shaded area shown in Fig. 50(b).

Equating the two expressions for V we obtain,

$$(h_o - h)A = \frac{1}{r} \int_0^t h dt$$

MODELS

and writing $T = Ar$ (the time-constant of the system) we have

$$h_o - h = \frac{1}{T} \int_0^t h\,dt$$

or

$$h = h_o - \frac{1}{T} \int_0^t h\,dt$$

The signal flowgraph which corresponds to this equation is shown in Fig. 51(a) and (b). Note particularly the negative feedback inherent in the system. This example illustrates the point

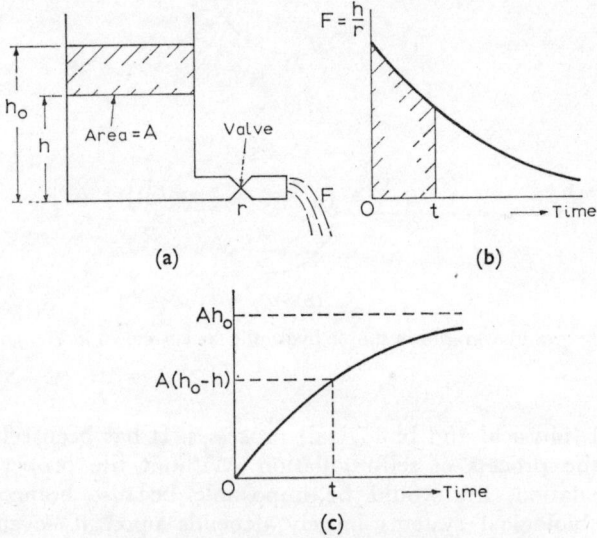

Fig. 50. Behaviour of a simple hydraulic model

made previously that the signal flowgraph brings out the dynamic structure of a system by stressing the dependencies which exist between key variables.

Let us examine in a little more detail the "inherent negative feedback" link shown in Fig. 51(a) and in the equivalent flowgraph of Fig. 51(b). Clearly, no physical information feedback channel appears explicitly in the system under consideration, as shown in Fig. 50(a). But, on the other hand, there is a relationship between the height (h) of the liquid and the rate of change of height. Or, expressed in another way, a relationship exists between the height (h) of liquid at time t and the total volume of liquid (V) which has been discharged from the tank during the period $t = 0$ to t seconds. It is this relationship which gives rise to the negative feedback configuration shown in Fig. 51(a). It exemplifies an important property inherent in many

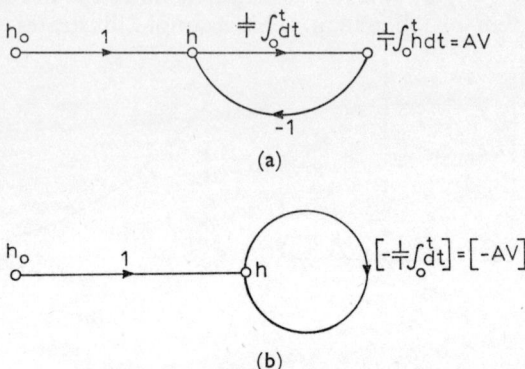

Fig. 51. Flowgraphs of simple hydraulic system shown in Fig. 50

natural (physical and biological) processes. It has been referred to as the process of self-regulation. Without the property of self-regulation, life would be impossible because homeostasis in all biological systems largely depends upon it—even the weather is a self-regulating process. The reader will no doubt think of many other classes of self-regulating systems which occur in nature.

The phenomenon of exponential decay has been treated in some detail because of its fundamental importance in the study of all classes of information feedback control systems, and because of its intrinsic importance in nature.

It is interesting to compare the signal flowgraph of the system with self-regulatory characteristics, considered above, with that of the elementary closed-loop system, considered previously, and shown in Fig. 44. The corresponding mathematical model is defined by the two relationships,

$$e = x_i - x_o$$
$$x_o = Ke$$

In this model x_i is the input signal, x_o is the output signal, e is the error signal and K is the gain factor. The model corresponds

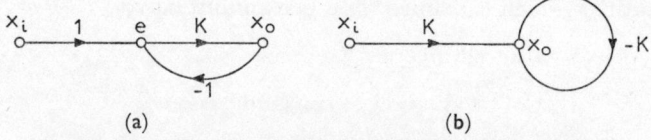

(a) (b)

Fig. 52. Equivalent flowgraphs of idealized negative feedback control system

to a highly idealized system. The corresponding signal flowgraph, shown in two equivalent forms, is given in Fig. 52(a) and (b). The relationship between x_o and x_i is

$$x_o = \frac{K}{1 + K} \cdot x_i$$

If, instead of a negative feedback system, we had considered a positive feedback system, the relationship between x_o and x_i would become,

$$x_o = \frac{K}{1 - K} \cdot x_i$$

and, as shown in Fig. 53, the self-loop operator of the positive feedback system is $+K$.

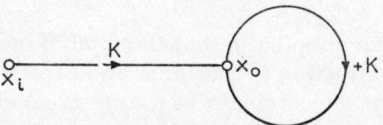

Fig. 53. Flowgraph of idealized positive feedback system

The flowgraph method of depicting the mathematical model of a system has universal application. Consider, for example, an idealized model of an economic system. It is a simplified version of an economic model originally devised by Lord Keynes. It is based on a model which, incidentally, has proved most effective in the economic planning of several nations including the United States. The model is introduced merely to demonstrate that the flowgraph technique can be useful in the study of all systems in which we can define relationships between the key variables.

In the simplified economic model we define the following quantities—each is defined on a per annum basis:

$Y =$ total of all incomes,

$P =$ cost of production of consumer goods,

$I =$ cost of production of capital goods—this may be regarded as a rate of investment,

$C =$ money spent on purchase of consumer goods,

$S =$ savings.

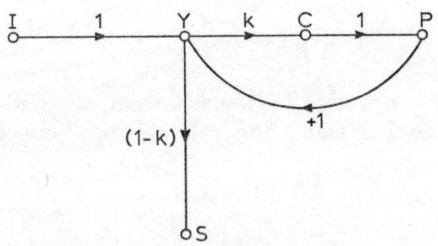

Fig. 54. Flowgraph of a simple economic model based on Keynes' model

We assume, for simplicity, that the total of incomes is the sum of the cost of production of consumer and capital goods, and that the money spent on purchases of consumer goods is a fraction k of the total of incomes. We can also equate P, the money spent on the production of consumer goods, with C, the money spent on the purchase of consumer goods. Our simple mathematical model of this steady-state economic system reduces to the following relationships:

$$Y = I + P,$$
$$C = kY,$$
$$P = C,$$
$$S = (1 - k)Y.$$

The flowgraph corresponding to this mathematical model is shown in Fig. 54. From our present point of view an important characteristic of the system is that it embodies positive feedback. The flowgraph shows up the structure of the system in a unique way. Indeed, economists are already beginning to apply the flowgraph technique to complex economic systems, and to use general-purpose electronic computers to study the effects of various economic policies.

Application of Flowgraphs to Solution of Algebraic Equations

Although the flowgraph method is not recommended as a method for solving simultaneous algebraic equations it may nevertheless be used for this purpose.

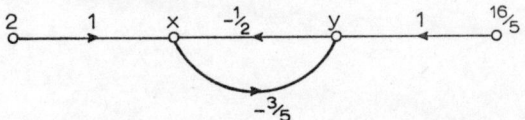

Fig. 55. Flowgraph for pair of simultaneous algebraic equations

Suppose we require the solution of the pair of simultaneous algebraic equations:
$$4x + 2y = 8,$$
$$3x + 5y = 16.$$

The equations can be rewritten in the form:
$$x = \frac{8 - 2y}{4} = 2 - \frac{y}{2}$$
$$y = \frac{16 - 3x}{5} = \frac{16}{5} - \frac{3}{5}x$$

and the corresponding flowgraph is shown in Fig. 55. Using the transformation process used previously for replacing a feedback loop by a single branch and a self-loop, Fig. 55 can be transformed into Fig. 56. The value of x can then be determined directly from the flowgraph as follows:

$$x = (1) \cdot 2 + \left(-\frac{1}{2}\right) \cdot \frac{16}{5} + \frac{3}{10} x$$

$$\frac{7}{10} x = 2 - \frac{16}{10} = \frac{4}{10}$$

$$x = \frac{4}{7}$$

Hence we can obtain y,

$$y = \frac{16}{5} - \frac{12}{35} = \frac{20}{7}.$$

This method of solving a pair of simultaneous algebraic equations is obviously clumsy and certainly not as convenient

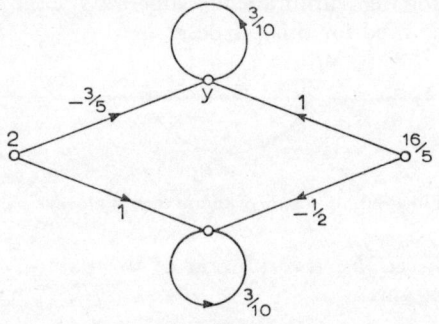

Fig. 56. Transformed flowgraph equivalent to Fig. 55

as the straightforward algebraic method. But it is fun, because it is different. And it is important to note that if the equations had been a pair of differential equations the flowgraph treatment, outlined above, would lead directly to an analogue computer programme for the solution of the equations.

The point I want to stress is that the development of a flowgraph emphasizes the structure of a mathematical model in a way that facilitates understanding of the process under consideration, and it often helps appreciably in programming a computer.

Insofar as the solution of higher order systems of simultaneous algebraic equations is concerned, a reduction technique, known as the "loop rule", has been developed. It provides a rapid means of reducing the corresponding flowgraph, and hence of obtaining the solutions of the set of equations. The method closely parallels Cramer's well-known method for reducing determinants.

Models as Controllers

Models lend themselves admirably to the study of automatic control systems, especially when it is necessary to explore the effect of changes in an appreciable number of control parameters. Their merit is due to the fact that a process or machine can be simulated, using a speeded-up time scale, so that the exploration of many system modifications can be undertaken in minimum time.

In some control problems, moreover, it is convenient to use models in an actual controlling role. If, for example, we build a true-time model of a process and decide that the characteristics of the model are those which we desire in the process itself, in spite of the influence of outside disturbances, we can sometimes use the model to constrain the actual system to give the desired behaviour by using the arrangement shown schematically in Fig. 57. The input to the model is identical with the input to the system. But when the behaviour of the system differs from the desired behaviour, which is in fact the output of the model (indicated by P in the diagram), the difference is added to the input signal and the combined signal provides the input to the process. It can be shown, although it is beyond our present scope, that the model-controlled system, shown in Fig. 57, is usually stable and gives high-speed performance. The unstabilizing influence of measuring delays, and other delays in the process, is balanced out by similar delays which are built into the model. In the next chapter we shall consider the effect of such delays on the stability of simple closed-loop systems.

It is worth noting that the use of models as "on-line process controllers" is an exemplification of the principle of the optimum utilization of information which was introduced earlier. Incidentally, "on-line operation" implies the use of a computer, or model, continually in the operation of a process. We consider the computer to be an integral part of the system being controlled. The term "optimum utilization of information" implies that, by

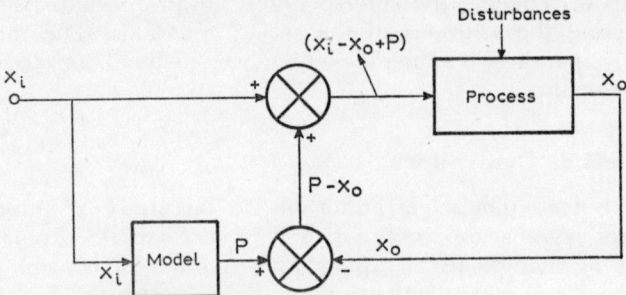

Fig. 57. Principle of the model controller

monitoring the past behaviour of a process, we assemble adequate data to build a realistic model of the system. Having built the model the remaining uncertainty in the behaviour of the process is due to the effect of outside disturbances (which are usually beyond our control). The net effect is that the overall uncertainty in the operation of the system is reduced by using the model as a controller and, although a closed cycle of operations is still necessary, the possibility of sustained oscillations being excited may be appreciably reduced.

6. Stability

Sometimes, when the wind is light, I crew for a friend in his sailing dinghy. Because I am a novice, I frequently have the impression that the boat is in a precarious state and that even a moderate gust of wind might capsize it. It feels unstable. On the other hand an experienced sailor welcomes sprightly behaviour in his craft and rejoices in being able to stabilize it, in the sense of keeping the mast upright, in comparatively high winds and rough conditions. The dinghy sailor uses a combination of sail settings, helm, centre-board, and ever-changing positions of his centre of gravity, relative to the centre of gravity of the boat, to achieve stability. I would be very surprised if even the most sophisticated digital computer could achieve the same result and win races into the bargain!

In nature, and in man-made machines and processes, continuous struggles are waged to maintain stability of biological systems, of economic systems, and of physical systems because an unstable state is usually undesirable and often leads to disaster. Examples are common. For example, disease is often a manifestation of unstable behaviour in biological systems of all classes—rapid fluctuations in body temperature, or blood pressure, or blood sugar, etc. correspond to unstable conditions and are symptomatic of some disease or other. Similarly, fluctuations of increasing magnitude in the value of a nation's currency are evidence of the nation's poor economic health. A child, learning to ride a bicycle, may experience several falls before mastering the complex balancing and steering operations required to achieve stability. We know that, when controlled by a beginner, a bicycle, or car, may be a highly unstable entity.

In this chapter we will consider the nature of stability, and instability, some of the reasons for unstable behaviour, and some methods of counteracting tendencies towards instability. Instability is essentially, but not uniquely, a characteristic of systems which incorporate information feedback, and hence its special place in this book. First, let us define stability as it is understood by physical scientists and engineers.

Stability is a characteristic of a process, machine, or system whose response to an external, or internal disturbance, dies down when the stimulus is removed. On the other hand if, after the application of the disturbance, the process or machine continues to oscillate with constant or increasing amplitude, after the removal of the disturbance, we say that the process is unstable. Alternatively, a process may be unstable if its response to a disturbance continues to grow, perhaps exponentially, after the disturbance is removed. A rock, balanced precariously at the edge of a cliff, is a good example of the latter condition.

If I suddenly change the setting of a domestic thermostat from, say, $65°F$ to $75°F$ the temperature of my home or office will eventually settle down to a value which fluctuates between perhaps $74\frac{1}{2}°F$ and $75\frac{1}{2}°F$. As explained in Chapter 4 such a fluctuation is characteristic of on-off control systems like the thermostatic control, and the system is considered to be stable. Similarly, if I suddenly displace the control lever, controlling the angle of elevation of a large optical, or radio telescope, the axis of the telescope may overshoot slightly the desired elevation angle, but normally the servomechanism will be sufficiently well stabilized to bring the telescope to rest comparatively quickly. The telescope control system is said to be stable.

But if excessively long exponential time delays, or for that matter finite time delays, are involved in the measurement of angular misalignment, or in the application of the desired correcting forces, or torques, and if, in addition, the gain of the amplifier (which determines the speed of response) is set too high, there is a fair probability of unstable behaviour arising. The same kind of conditions may lead to instability in economic and biological systems. In an economic system, for example, if unnecessarily long delays are involved in the decision-making process and if, subsequently, excessive remedial action is taken (i.e. the "gain" is too high), there is a fair probability that economic instability will arise. Similarly, in some biological systems, if the central nervous system and the brain do not receive vital information concerning body malfunction sufficiently quickly and then over-compensate the deficiency or malfunction, a state of shock and accompanying instability may arise.

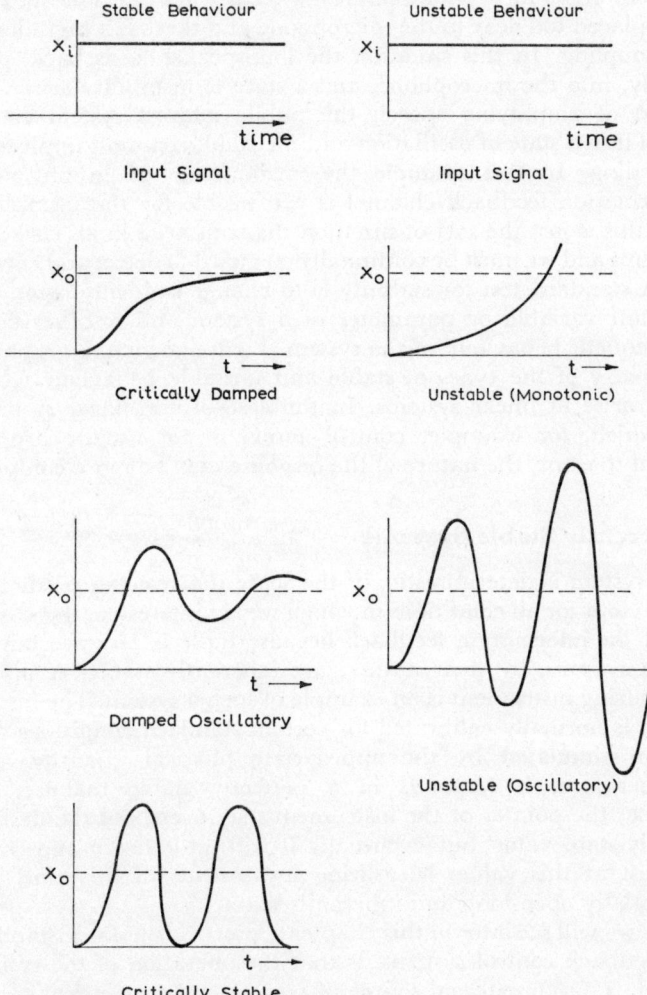

Fig. 58. Stable and unstable behaviour in linear systems

An excellent example of unstable behaviour in a feedback system arises in a public address system when the loudspeakers are placed too near to the microphone and there is a high degree of coupling. In this situation the loudspeaker feeds back, positively, into the microphone, and a state of instability arises. Instead of amplifying speech the public address system excites itself into a state of oscillation and the result is a most unpleasant whistling. In this example the introduction of an unwanted information feedback channel is responsible for the instability. But this is just the sort of situation that can arise in all classes of systems and we must be continually on guard to detect and correct it. A standard test for stability is to change suddenly some important variable or parameter of a system and to observe the subsequent behaviour of the system. Figure 58 gives a graphical summary of the types of stable and unstable behaviour which may arise in linear systems. In the case of non-linear systems, in which, for example, control action is not usually proportional to error, the nature of the response may be more complex.

Inherently Stable Systems

If a system is deterministic, in the sense that we can predict its behaviour for all conditions in which we are interested, there is no need for information feedback because there is no uncertainty. Such systems, by their nature, are inherently stable. A simple measuring instrument is an example of such a system. The instrument is normally calibrated for certain standard conditions and when stimulated by the appropriate physical quantity, e.g. temperature, it responds in a perfectly stable manner. Of course, the pointer of the instrument may overshoot the desired steady-state value but eventually it will settle down and come to rest at this value. Measuring instruments of this kind are essentially open-loop and inherently stable.

As we will see later in this chapter a prerequisite for instability in feedback control systems, is that the operation of the system depends on an external source of power—in an electrical servomechanism, for example, the source of power is often the a.c. mains supply. But open, or closed, loop systems in which no external source of power is involved can be assumed to be inherently stable. Further, the majority of programmed control systems are inherently stable. An important class of programmed system, in which feedback may be incorporated, is the program of a digital computer.

In view of the importance of computer programming, and as an illustration of the essentially feedback character of the iterative process in programming, we will consider the almost trivial problem of determining the largest common divisor of two positive numbers a and b. One way of solving the problem is to carry out a series of subtractions until the subtrahend and the remainder are the same number as illustrated in the numerical example below.

Suppose the two numbers are $a = 216$ and $b = 81$. We proceed as follows:

Step 1	$a \neq b$	a	216	Minuend
		b	81	Subtrahend
		c	135	Remainder
Step 2	$b \neq c$	c	135	
		b	81	Subtrahend
		d	54	Remainder
Step 3	$b \neq d$	b	81	
		d	54	Subtrahend
			27	Remainder
Step 4	$d \neq e$	d	54	
		e	27	Subtrahend
		f	27	Remainder
Step 5	$e = f$			

The largest common divisor of 216 and 81 is 27.

A computer flow diagram for the process is shown in Fig. 59. The significant operational blocks are designated I, II, ..., V. The diagram illustrates the operations involved in step (1). Note that operation III computes the modulus (the value irrespective of the sign of a number—the modulus of −64 is 64) of the difference $(a - b)$; it is written $|(a - b)|$. The cycle is then repeated after replacing "a" by $|(a - b)|$, operation II being carried out to check for equality and then proceeding as shown in

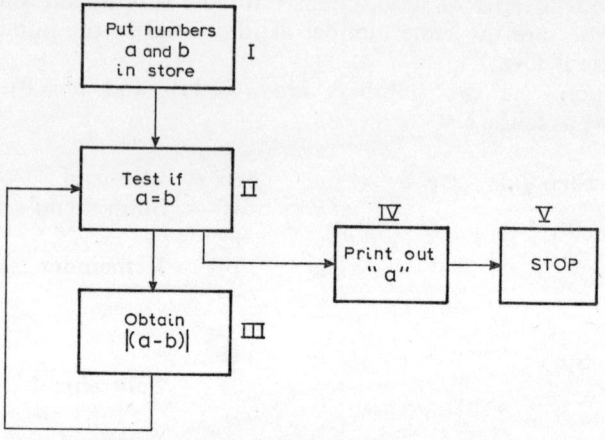

Fig. 59. Computer flow diagram for determination of largest common divisor of two numbers a and b

the diagram. The process continues to cycle until the subtrahend and the remainder at, say, step j are equal. In the numerical example this occurs at step (4) and the computation is stopped at the beginning of step (5). The process is inherently stable, since the sequence of "remainders", except in the special case when $a = b$, consists of a sequence of smaller and smaller numbers. In an unstable system, the numbers would become progressively larger and larger.

Another class of inherently stable closed-loop system is that which incorporates, within the closed loop, only one or two exponential delays. A closed-loop which includes one exponential delay is normally described as a first-order system and a closed-loop with two exponential delays is described as a second-order control system—the corresponding mathematical models are a first and a second-order differential equation respectively. A third, or higher, order control system may in some circumstances be unstable. Often the term "unstable" is used loosely to describe systems which have an oscillatory, or "hunting", response as shown in Fig. 58(c). This meaning of the term does not line up with the definition given previously, nor is it accepted by scientists and engineers. Nevertheless it is important, when talking about instability, to state unambiguously what we mean by the term "unstable system". This I have attempted to do. But there are some systems, usually incorporating several interconnected closed-loops, which behave as unstable systems until a final "outside loop" is closed when stable behaviour is immediately induced. We say that the open-loop response of the system is unstable but that the closed-loop response is stable. The stability of such systems, assuming linear behaviour, can be tested using the famous Nyquist stability criterion.

A Model for Demonstrating Stability and Instability

It was pointed out earlier that a closed-loop system may be unstable if the amplification, or gain, in the loop is sufficiently high, and if there is excessive delay in transmitting a signal around the loop. To demonstrate how amplification and time-lags affect the behaviour of control systems which involve closed-loops, I have devised a simple model to demonstrate their effects.

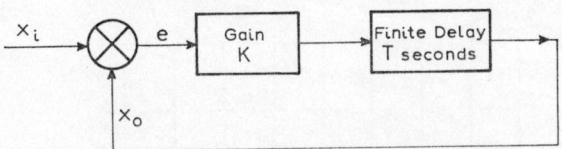

Fig. 60. A model for demonstrating stability

It should be stressed that this model has no practical significance, although similar systems were used in the early days of computer development as so-called delay-line storage systems.

The model is shown schematically in Fig. 60. It involves an input signal x_i, and output signal x_o, which is fed back negatively and compared with the input signal to form the signal $e = (x_i - x_o)$ and, within the closed loop, it includes an amplifier (gain K) and a finite delay-line which introduces a T seconds delay. The finite-time delay element may be composed of a large number of single exponential delay elements in series.

Suppose the input signal (x_i) is as shown in Fig. 61(a). We will consider the behaviour of this hypothetical control system

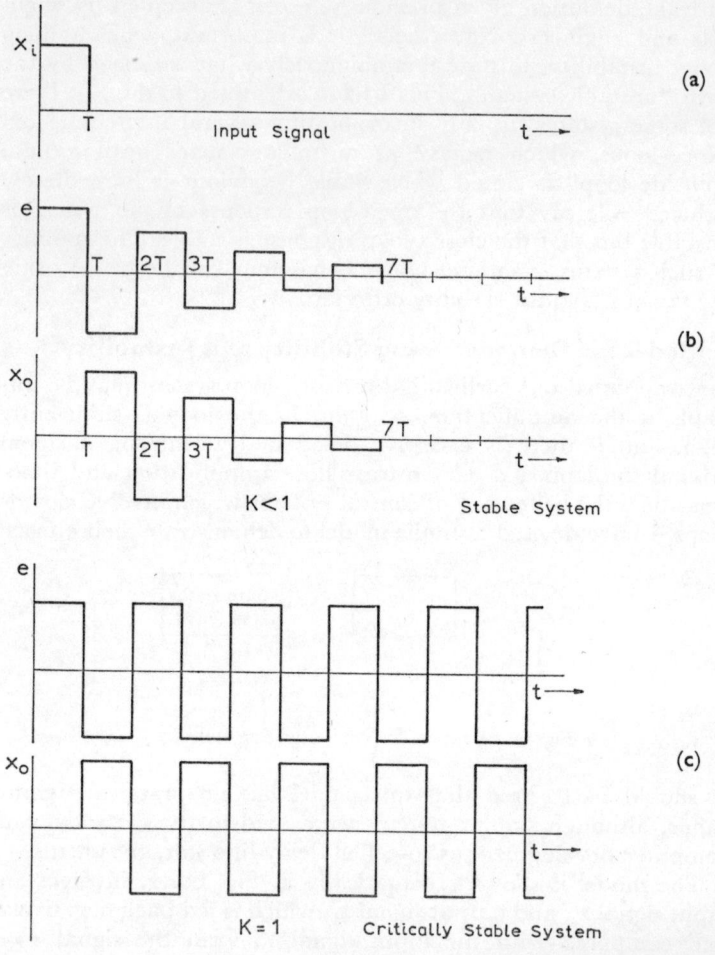

Fig. 61 part

STABILITY

for values of K, the amplification factor, less than, equal to, and greater than unity.

It is convenient to develop the response of the system diagrammatically as shown in Fig. 61(b), (c), and (d). The diagrams

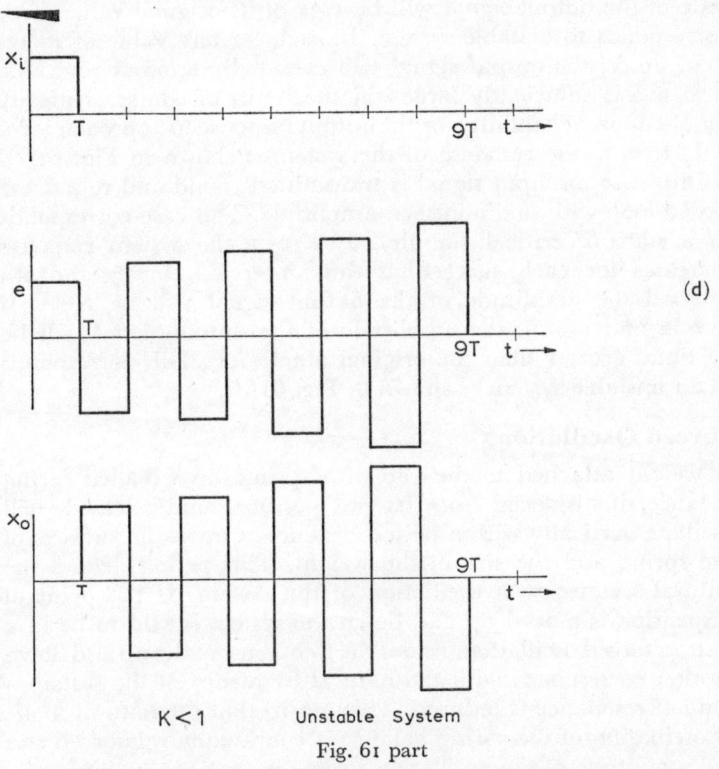

K < 1   Unstable System

Fig. 61 part

are self-explanatory. The input signal x_i, during the first interval of time T, gives rise to an error signal e of the same amplitude and duration because during this period the output signal x_o is zero. During the time period T to $2T$ the output signal x_o has an amplitude smaller than the amplitude of the corresponding error signal because K is less than 1. This output signal gives rise to an error signal of opposite polarity but of the same amplitude and duration. Since, after the initial time interval T, the input signal is zero, we find that after nT seconds (say during the nth interval) the amplitude of the output signal will be reduced by a factor K^{n-1}. If, for example, $K = \frac{1}{2}$ and $n = 6$, the amplitude of the output signal will be 1/32 of its original value. This corresponds to a stable system. Indeed, for any value of K less than unity, the output signal will eventually approach a value zero if n is sufficiently large—in the limit, of course, n ideally should approach infinity for the output response to approach zero.

If $K = 1$, the response of the system is shown in Fig. 61(c). In this case an input signal is transmitted round and round the closed loop with undiminished amplitude. This case corresponds to a state of critical stability. If $K > 1$ the system response increases for each succeeding time interval. During the nth interval the amplitude of the output signal will be K^{n-1}. If $K = 2$ and $n = 6$, the amplitude of the output signal will be 32 times greater than the original amplitude. This corresponds to an unstable system as shown in Fig. 61(d).

Forced Oscillations

A weight attached to the end of a spring, or a loaded spring balance, if displaced from its rest position, and released, will oscillate vertically with a period dependent upon the stiffness of the spring and the size of the weight. This period defines the natural frequency of oscillation of the system. If the point of suspension is moved up and down the system is said to be in a state of forced oscillation. And if the frequency of the up and down motion corresponds with the natural frequency of the system a state of resonance is induced. This means that the natural mode of oscillation of the spring balance is continually reinforced and the amplitude of the oscillation increases continually. Similarly, if the model used to demonstrate stability, see Fig. 60, is excited by a sequence of square pulses of the form shown in Fig. 61(c) (rather than a single pulse as used in the previous experiment) it is readily demonstrated that, for $K = 1$, the output will consist of a sequence of pulses which progressively double in amplitude from one pulse to the next. The system is in a condition of resonance and incidentally of instability. The dynamic equivalence between the spring balance and the model will be noted.

STABILITY

During the past fifty years research workers in acoustics and electrical communications have been deeply concerned with the forced oscillations of acoustical and electronic systems. The type of experiment used in so-called frequency response studies is illustrated in Fig. 62(a). We assume an electrical system. A train of constant frequency, constant amplitude, sinusoidal signals is applied to the input of the system, or instrument, and the corresponding amplitude and phase shift of the output signal is measured and compared with the amplitude and phase

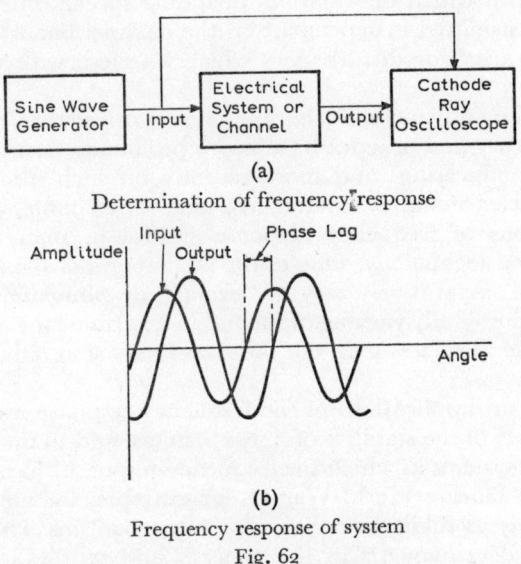

(a)
Determination of frequency response

(b)
Frequency response of system
Fig. 62

of the input signal. A cathode ray tube is a convenient instrument to use in the experiment because a direct visual comparison of the input and output signals can be obtained. A typical result is shown in Fig. 62(b). If a range of values of frequency of the input signal is used, and we determine the corresponding output behaviour of the system the frequency response characteristics of the system can be deduced. If, for each value of frequency, the output frequency is the same as the input frequency we conclude that the system is linear.

The frequency response characteristic of a system is defined in terms of the ratio of the output signal amplitude to the input signal amplitude, and the corresponding phase shift, for a range of input frequencies. The amplitude ratio is sometimes referred to as the "gain" of the system. Of particular interest to communications engineers is the band-width of a channel or instrument. It is obtained directly from the frequency response characteristic—it can be defined as the range of frequencies which are transmitted by the channel without attenuation. The degree of fidelity with which information, including speech, music, video, etc. is transmitted is dependent on the channel band-width and on the "noise" or disturbances which interfere with the transmission.

The many advances, during the present century, in communication theory and practice have had a profound effect on control systems engineering, and more recently on such disciplines as medical science and economics. We find, for example, increasing applications of frequency response studies in many fields of science and technology. One of the advantages of the method is that it is comparatively easy to "excite", or stimulate, a system using a sinusoidally varying input and to determine the amplitude and phase displacement of the resulting sinusoidal output signal.

Important applications of the frequency response method are to the study of the stability of linear systems, and to the synthesis of control systems in which the frequency-response characteristics are given. During World War II, for example, the method was particularly useful in the design of servomechanisms. The massive war-time developments in the analysis and synthesis of linear servomechanisms clearly paved the way for the spectacular achievements in the field of automatic control which we have witnessed during the past ten years.

In the determination of the frequency-response of servomechanisms, if the amplitude of the output sinusoidal signal is more than twice that of the amplitude of the input sinusoidal signal, we usually decide that the behaviour of the system, under normal operating conditions, will be too oscillatory. In a practical system it will be necessary to introduce more damping into the system. We consider below some standard methods for stabilizing closed-loop systems.

Methods of Stabilization

The torsion pendulum experiments described previously may be regarded as a means of simulating the behaviour of second-order servomechanisms and automatic regulators. It was shown that, by increasing the viscous damping coefficient of the system, the degree of oscillation subsequent to an initial displacement could be reduced.

But the more we increase the viscous damping coefficient, the more we increase the tendency of the system to lag when a constant angular velocity input is applied. Suppose, for instance, the suspended system, of the torsion pendulum, Fig. 45, is rotated with constant angular velocity about the point of suspension P. We let the tank containing damping liquid remain stationary, and, for this experiment, let the scale be attached rigidly to the suspension clamp P so that it rotates as P rotates. We find, after the equilibrium state is reached, that the pointer position is displaced from the zero reading by an amount proportional to the rate of rotation of the system. Furthermore, the more viscous the damping liquid, or the deeper the can is inserted into the damping liquid, the greater the displacement of the pointer from the zero position. When the constant angular rotation is stopped the pointer returns to the zero position (the approach is approximately simple exponential if m is small and B is large).

The displacement of the pointer corresponds to what we refer to as the "steady-state velocity lag" of the system which, as the name implies, is proportional to velocity. The torsion pendulum system demonstrates, for example, that if we increase the viscous damping associated with the output member of a control system, in order to damp out undesirable oscillations of the system, a direct consequence is that the dynamic lag, which arises when the output tries to follow a constant velocity input, increases.

If viscous damping is introduced to reduce the oscillatory behaviour of high-power servomechanisms another disadvantage of the method is apparent. Work must be performed to rotate a viscous damping system (e.g. a cylinder rotating in a viscous liquid), and this is non-useful work. It is in fact dissipated in heat. Although the effect can be ignored in the case of low-power servos it may be appreciable if we rely on added viscous damping to stabilize, say, a servomechanism which incorporates a 1000 h.p. motor.

The conclusion is that, although increasing the viscous friction coefficient always reduces the oscillatory behaviour of a linear servomechanism, it has the double disadvantage of (*a*) introducing larger dynamic errors in the system and (*b*) wasting energy. Nor is it always convenient to compensate dynamic lag by introducing integral of error control. Accordingly, we must seek more efficient methods of stabilizing servomechanisms and automatic control systems in general. Perhaps the most profitable approach to the problem of stabilizing a control system, embodying information feedback, is to modify the correction signal in order to take into account the rate of change of the error itself. The method is called "derivative of error stabilization". But this somewhat sophisticated terminology merely obscures what is essentially a common-sense approach to the problem.

Let me describe the method by using, as an example, the task of the pilot of an aircraft in carrying out an instrument landing in low visibility conditions. The problem will, of necessity, be oversimplified but it nevertheless exemplifies the idea of stabilizing a control system by changing the nature of the controlling signal. In principle, the instrument landing system requires the pilot to line up his aircraft with radio beams which define the desired flight path. The system, shown in the form of a simplified block diagram, in Fig. 63, is complex, and we need concern ourselves only with the visual display which provides the pilot with information relating to the displacement of the aircraft from the beam.* The display system normally consists of a cathode ray tube over the surface of which a graticule is superposed as shown in Fig. 64. The display indicates the displacement of the aircraft from the desired flight path—for simplicity only the horizontal displacement will be considered.

When correctly aligned the cathode ray beam is focused at the centre of the cathode ray tube as shown in Fig. 64(*a*). If the aircraft is to the left of the radio beam, as shown in Fig. 64(*b*), a turn to the right is required to bring the aircraft into the flight path, while, if the aircraft is displaced to the right of the beam, a turn to the left is required.

* In practice the pilot receives both visual and auditory information concerning the relative positions of the aircraft and the beam.

STABILITY

If the displacement of the cathode ray spot from the centre of the tube depends only on the displacement of the aircraft from the radio beam considerable skill is required on the part of the pilot to prevent the aircraft from oscillating about the beam.

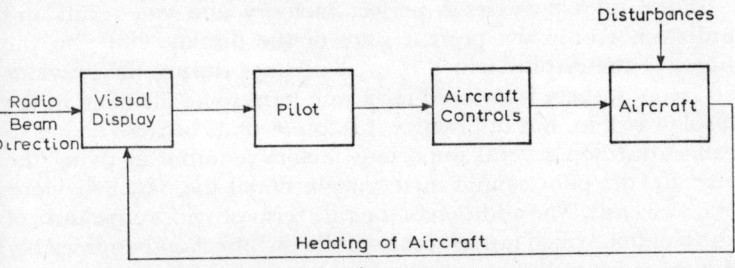

Fig. 63. Block diagram of aircraft blind-landing system

On account of the inherent delays between joystick movement and the corresponding change in aircraft heading, the system may be difficult to stabilize. But if the "error signal", shown on the cathode ray tube, is a combination of the actual displacement of the aircraft from the beam plus (or minus) a measure of the rate at which

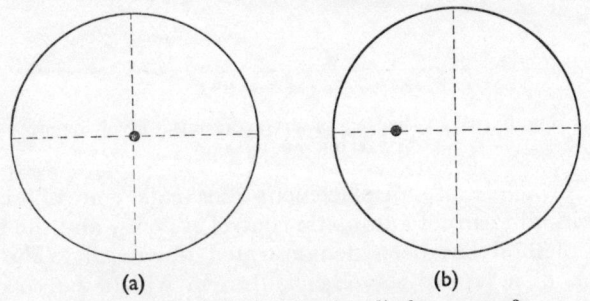

Fig. 64. Visual display showing displacement of aircraft from radio beam

the aircraft is moving away from the beam (or approaching the beam) we have, in effect, introduced information into the display which adds a degree of anticipation into the system. For example, with the modified display, if the aircraft crosses the beam from right to left, in spite of a small lateral displacement, the rate of departure from the beam may be appreciable, and the pilot will observe a comparatively large "error signal" to the left, and he will take appropriate corrective action. Alternatively, if the aircraft is an appreciable distance to the right of the beam but is approaching the beam fairly rapidly, the pilot may observe only a small error to the right.

If the pilot possesses a perfect memory and can recall and utilize, not only the present state of the display, but also the states of the display which existed perhaps during the previous 60 seconds, there is no need for a rate term to be included in the display system. But in practice it is found that, because he has to concentrate on several important factors required in flying the aircraft, the pilot cannot memorize in detail the past behaviour of his aircraft. The addition of the rate term provides a measure of anticipation which introduces a stabilizing effect and appreciably simplifies his task.

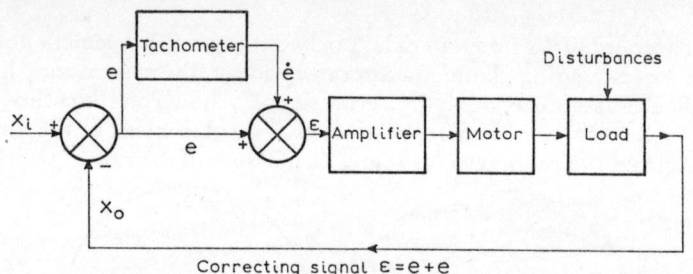

Fig. 65. Block diagram of servomechanism involving an error rate term

The principle of "displacement plus rate control" is used widely in all forms of automatic control systems, and the success of the method has been demonstrated universally. The block diagram of a typical servomechanism in which the correcting force, or torque, tending to restore the system to the desired state, depends on the magnitude of the error, plus a term dependent on the rate of change of error, is shown in Fig. 65. A tachometer measures the rate of change of error, and the "rate" signal $\dot{e}$ is added to e. An important point to note is that, in contrast with the addition of viscous damping, as a stabilizing means, the introduction of an error rate term into the controller has no effect on the dynamic lags inherent in the system nor does it waste energy.

As mentioned previously the stabilization of control systems by introducing an error rate term represents the commonsense approach. When I drive a car, or ride a bicycle, my brain continually anticipates what may happen next and, in doing so, account is continually being taken of rates of change of error, and even of rates of rates of change of the error signals. Without anticipation of this kind it would be impossible for us to continue to live because we would find ourselves in a state of continuous instability which would lead inevitably to the extinction of life.

Another commonsense method of dealing with oscillatory behaviour is to reduce the amplification or "gain" in the closed-loop of operations. Clearly, if the corrective action is slowed down, there is less chance of the control motors keeping up with high rates of change of input and using this method, it is inevitable that the speed of response of the system will be reduced. In practice, good design of control systems necessitates the achievement of a compromise between adequate speed of response and adequate damping of oscillations—these are generally incompatible requirements. But the selection of an appropriate amplification factor, combined with an appropriate level of error rate control usually produces a satisfactory result.

The use of models as controllers, as mentioned in Chapter 5, is another approach to the problem of achieving high speed of response without impairing stable performance. What we try to do in this approach to the problem is to attempt to replace a closed-loop system by an open-loop system. Unfortunately the technique has limited application. If a moral can be drawn from the stability story it is that the more effectively we can apply known information, past and present, in the control of any process or machine, the more effectively we will control that process or machine.

Biological Systems

From time to time in this book I have referred to biological control processes. Of all control processes known to man the fantastic network of interconnected neurons in the brain, the communicating nerve fibres, the countless chemical reactions, and the vast array of human muscles all together constitute by many orders of magnitude the most complex system with which man is confronted. How this system manages to be self-stabilizing in the presence of a multiplicity of disturbances of all kinds, including severe brain damage, is far beyond the present status of control theory to explain. Even the most powerful modern computer can simulate only a minute fragment of this unbelievably complex system.

But this does not imply that the principles of feedback as applied, for example, in physical control systems have not helped the biological scientist to understand more adequately certain biological processes. It is now universally accepted, for instance, that negative feedback plays an indispensable role in the majority of biological processes. And the maintenance of homeostasis, and indeed the maintenance of purposeful activity in the biological world, may be thought of in much the same way as we think of goal-directed servomechanisms. Norbert Wiener, the founder of cybernetics, was undoubtedly influenced by certain biological conditions when he formulated the scope of the subject. One such condition, described as "cerebellar attaxia", the major symptom of which is a continuous trembling of a patient's limbs, was explained by Wiener as an unstable condition brought about by malfunctioning of negative feedback paths. He based this conclusion on the fact that the majority of patients suffering from this condition possessed healthy kinaesthetic sensors, motor nerves, and muscles.

Control of the limbs is accomplished by muscles, excited by motor neurons, the response of which is monitored by special nerve cells—the resultant information is fed back to the spinal chord and the brain. If this closed cycle of operations is impaired—in the doctor's office it is checked by exciting, for example, the knee jerk by a gently applied "hammer" blow in the correct place—there is a possibility that oscillatory behaviour might result. The regulatory systems involved in body function, and more especially in the functioning of such complex systems as the cardio-vascular system, and the respiratory system, are probably hierarchical in character. This means that one closed-loop monitors the performance of an inner loop, which monitors the performance of another inner loop, and so on. But the nature of the stabilization techniques are not known. This is understandable when we consider that many interacting variables are involved and most of the systems are non-linear.

One test of a well-designed servomechanism is to determine

how precisely it will follow a very slowly changing input signal. As the velocity of the input shaft is decreased there is an increasing tendency for the motion of the output shaft to become discontinuous in the sense of being "stop-go". Human limbs satisfy this test to an extraordinary degree. I can move my hand, as it rests on a smooth surface, almost imperceptibly slowly without jerkiness. This suggests that the biological servomechanism controlling my hand is stabilized in a highly effective manner.

In spite of limited knowledge of the underlying principles involved in the stabilization of complex biological systems, there is increasing evidence that simplified dynamic models are helping medical science to understand the systemic aspects of the problem. And in turn this has given rise to more detailed formulations of some of the key control problems. Increasingly, the large-scale digital computer is being used to help the medical researcher track down the mechanisms of biological regulation, and in so doing it is providing a tool of outstanding potential for the conquest of disease.

7. The Learning Process

The learning process is God's greatest gift to man. One of the most thrilling experiences I can recall is the sight of my infant son in the early stages of conscious learning. It was his moment of truth when, after weeks of aimless rattling and prattling, he discovered, through some miraculous process, that shaking his rattle produced a sound. I remember the gleam in his eyes—the toothless grin. This was big stuff! And indeed it was—the very stuff of discovery. Triggered by his tactile, visual, and auditory sensors messages were being transmitted along nerve fibres to his brain, and in his brain associative links were set up which led to his discovery of the causal relationships between rattle, movement, and sound. Unwittingly he had completed successfully one of the most important experiments of his life. And it was largely through the information feedback process that the miracle had been achieved, because the whole process depended upon the feeding back of information to the visual, auditory and motor areas of the brain and upon the establishment of interconnecting pathways between them.

For centuries the learning process has fascinated man. It is more than 2300 years since the great Greek philosopher Aristotle studied the process of associative learning. There are two ways of answering the question—What is learning? First, in the everyday use of the word we think of it in terms of the acquisition of skills and habits—manipulative, intellectual or social. Second, from the point of view of the physiologist, learning is a process which causes certain organisms to undergo changes. These can be regarded as adaptive changes because they have been designed to safeguard life, to conserve energy, and to preserve a state of dynamic equilibrium in a changing and often unfavourable environment. However, neither the physiological nor the psychological implications of the learning process are fully understood. It will only be possible for us to look at some of the basic requirements in the process of learning and to see how important the feedback principle is in learning of all kinds. We assume that the long-term storage of information and data in the brain is a prerequisite to learning.

My main object in introducing the learning process in this book is not only to provide still another example of the universality of the feedback principle but, perhaps more important, to stimulate thinking about the subject. It is very clear, at present, that one of the most important processes all of us must be engaged in is the process of "learning how to learn". And I believe that this process will be facilitated if we have a rough idea of what we are trying to do. There seems to be general agreement, for example, that throughout his life man stores a vast array of habits the majority of which have been learned. These habits may be regarded as programmed controls which correspond approximately to computer programs insofar as the same set of input stimuli always produces the same set of responses. The human brain is, of course, continuously being re-programmed to deal with the uncertainties of life and to solve problems which have not been encountered previously. In this regard the learning capability of the brain far exceeds, by many orders of magnitude, that of the most powerful computer. This, in spite of the fact that within the last few years Dr. Arthur Samuel of the International Business Machines Corporation* has demonstrated that a computer can be programmed to play a fairly good game of draughts (checkers) through what can only be described as a learning process since the machine learns from past experience. But the basic rules of draughts are unambiguous and simple while the laws of nature and the laws of society are extremely complex.

It is important to note that the process of man's adaptation to the environment around him may be pre-programmed or may involve a learning process. Adaptive behaviour is of extraordinary complexity. One of the most simple examples of pre-programmed adaptation, for example, is the pupilliary contraction of the eye when a light is shone into it, or alternatively, the dilation of the pupil of the eye in a darkened room. Some of the basic requirements and mechanisms involved in the

---

* See, for example, "Electronic Computers", S. H. Hollingdale and G. C. Tootill, Pelican Book A524.

non-programmed adaptive process and in learning processes may be listed as:

(a) adequate memory and the ability to scan memory rapidly,
(b) information feedback channels in order to test the degree of success, or failure, of a particular action,
(c) the ability to classify information,
(d) the ability to recognize patterns, both deterministic and probabilistic,
(e) the ability to probe the environment by carrying out experiments and assessing the results,
(f) the ability to solve problems.

The adaptive and learning processes may be unconscious, as in the adjustment of our breathing rate to our rate of working, and the adjustment of our body temperature to external conditions, or, on the other hand, perceptive in which case the learning is a conscious process.

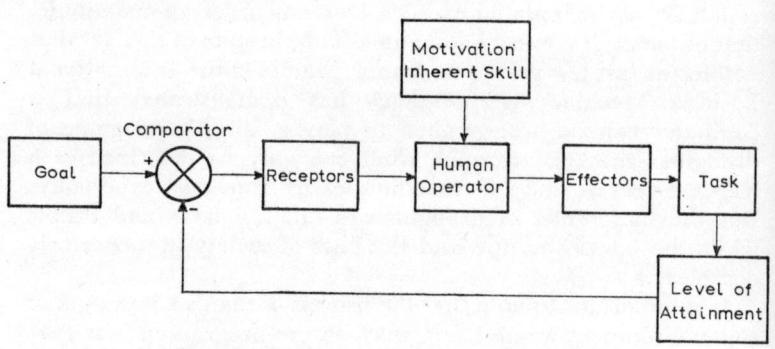

Fig. 66. Feedback nature of learning process

Trial and Error Learning

The learning process, when reduced to its fundamentals, may be represented schematically as in Fig. 66. Learning is necessarily a goal-seeking process and information feedback is inherent in it. In Fig. 66 it is assumed that a human operator is set a given task, perhaps an unfamiliar task, which involves consciousness. The learning process continues until, ideally, the operator's level of attainment approaches the goal set for the task. In some cases the goal is set in the brain of the operator, in other cases the goal is set by a teacher, an employer, a parent, etc. The level of attainment is monitored continuously and compared with the desired attainment level (the goal)—the difference between the two levels is used to enhance future performance. It is worth noting that we rarely perform a skill satisfactorily the first time we try it. But the more highly motivated we are, and the greater our skill-learning potential, in general, the more quickly we learn a new skill. Of great importance in learning is the "trial and error" process.

In the early 1900's the American psychologist E. L. Thorndike formulated the Law of Effect. This law embraces the important concept of "trial and error" learning—sometimes called "reinforcement learning".

When our response to a given situation, or a given problem, is successful the chances are that when the same situation, or problem, arises again our probability of success will be improved. And the more times the situation arises, the more likely it is that we will deal with it successfully. On the other hand, if our response turns out to be unsuccessful the chances that we will repeat it are diminished because we learn from experience. To explain this basic principle of "reinforcement learning" in terms of the known structure of the brain we might conclude that stimuli which produce successful responses, in the sense of responses which give pleasure, give rise to less and less "resistivity" in the "neural pathways" in the central nervous system. Alternatively, those stimuli which produce painful responses, when repeated, give rise to more and more resistivity in the neural pathways. This explanation of the mechanism of "trial and error" learning, although probably naive, at least provides a simple model upon which experiments and more sophisticated models can be based.

The trial and error learning process may be represented in block diagram form as shown in Fig. 67. Two major feedback loops are involved. In reality there may be many hundreds of feedback loops but to simplify the problem only two are considered. Both loops incorporate human receptors. We distinguish between them in a rather abstract way. For example, we regard loop I as being concerned with the immediate problem of carrying out the task to the required degree of perfection, while loop II may be regarded as the means whereby all information concerning the performance of the task, or of similar tasks, in the past, is stored and assessed. In other words the second loop establishes desirable neural paths and tends to inhibit undesirable paths. Loop II may accordingly be regarded as the learning loop and loop I as the loop which is responsible for carrying out the task as required.

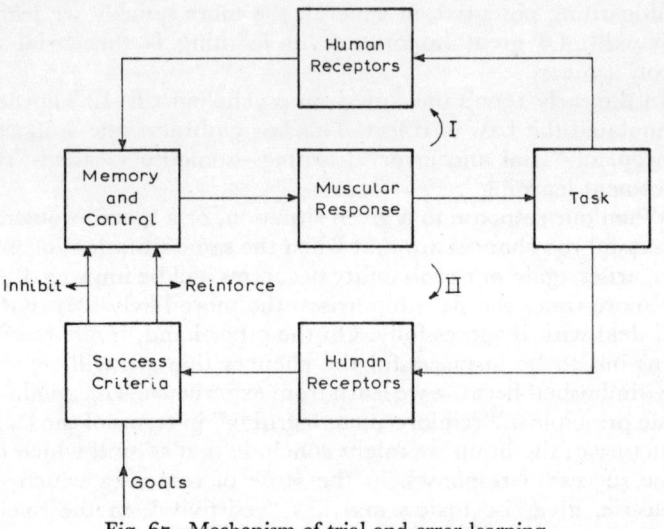

Fig. 67. Mechanism of trial and error learning

Many of the early experiments which gave rise to the concept of "trial and error" learning were based on animal behaviour. Thorndike showed that if a hungry cat is placed in a cage, the door of which will open only when the cat performs some simple task like depressing a lever, the cat will eventually reach food placed outside the cage. During the first experiment the cat will probably rush around the cage, frantically trying to escape, and eventually will probably accidentally depress the lever which opens the door. In the second experiment, and perhaps in the third and fourth and fifth experiments, the cat will display similar behaviour although gradually the time interval taken before the door is opened may tend to decrease. Perhaps during the next twenty trials there will be a noticeable decrease in the time taken for the cat to escape although even then behaviour will remain to some degree erratic. Eventually after perhaps forty or fifty trials the cat will have learned to depress the lever in order to achieve the desired result.

More recent experiments, involving trial and error learning, have been carried out using simple mazes. The animal, which is usually a rat, because rats display a marked degree of intelligence, explores the maze until the reward, in the form of food, is obtained. After running the maze more or less randomly during the first few trials, and eventually achieving success in each one, the rat gradually learns to select the shortest path to the reward. This it achieves essentially through a trial and error learning process. Although these experiments may appear to be trivial to most of us, they nevertheless have provided a wealth of knowledge concerning the learning process. For example, they have shown that learning is most effectively performed when the subject is highly motivated. For instance, a hungry rat will generally learn to find the reward more quickly than a rat which has just been fed. The same applies to humans. In general, the more motivated we are to learn a particular skill, the faster we will learn it. Looked at from the point of view of feedback control we might consider motivation as being related to the "gain" in the feedback loop. Successful moves which give rise to the reduction of error are more strongly reinforced the higher the gain in the system.

The trial and error learning process can, within limits, be mechanized. For example, a "mechanized rat" has been designed which learns to run a maze perfectly after a single trial run. The "rat" stores information relating to whether or not a particular turn leads to successfully reaching the goal or to a "blind alley". At the end of the trial run each possible turn is labelled "good" or "bad". In successive runs the "rat" ignores the "bad" turns and sequentially follows the "good" turns, until the goal is reached. Note that the trained "mechanical rat" will always reach the goal after the initial training run, but if the maze is changed it will still slavishly follow its original programme unless it is reprogrammed. On the other hand a live rat may take several trials to learn the maze but it will not be so helpless as the mechanized rat if the maze is changed.

In real life we rarely meet such simple situations as pre-programmed mazes which, once learned, can always be run satisfactorily. What happens is that we get involved in maze-like situations, and problems, but the mazes are non-static in the sense that they must be described in terms of probability laws rather than the laws of certainty. In other words, we are dealing with "stochastic" processes and the learning problem becomes a much greater challenge to our ingenuity and our creativity.

Several mechanized learning artefacts have been built. One of the best known was built by Dr. Grey Walter—it is called the "tortoise". The "tortoise" receives signals from its environment through photo-electric receptors and mechanical contact receptors. The "tortoise" can learn to move towards a light even when the light is moving and it can be inhibited from doing so when it receives inhibiting signals through the mechanical contact receptors. Its use to simulate a range of behaviour, previously thought to be uniquely characteristic of living animals, and insects, has been particularly interesting. But, to date, the work of Dr. Arthur Samuel in programming a general-purpose computer to learn to play a good game of draughts still ranks as the greatest achievement in the field of mechanized learning. Although programming a computer to learn to play a fair game of chess will be appreciably more difficult, and time consuming, there is no doubt that this will be achieved within the next decade. And perhaps within the next twenty-five years we will find chess-playing computers challenging the world's chess masters. In addition to being fun, the study of the learning process, by means of computer game-playing programs, is proving of immense value in such diverse areas as language translation by computers, the design of self-adaptive control systems, and the simulation of complex business games, to mention just a few.

Of fundamental importance in the process of learning is the requirement that a biological system, or a physical system, must be able to recognize patterns. The patterns we meet in everyday life are multitudinous and very diverse in nature. Some of them are considered later in this chapter. A prerequisite for pattern recognition is a capability to classify data.

Classification of Data

Have you ever pondered on how wonderfully equipped man is to classify and to recognize tens of thousands of entities with which he comes in contact? We can recognize faces even though we have not seen them for several years, and the slightest distortion of a TV picture is immediately recognized. In large measure the pattern recognition capability is due to our fabulous memory system and to its ability to classify objects, smells, feels of things, and so on. Let us consider as an example our ability to recognize substances by their smell. Although many animals have much greater sensitivity of smell, our capability in this respect is nevertheless impressive. It is perhaps second only in sensitivity to our fantastic sense of vision.

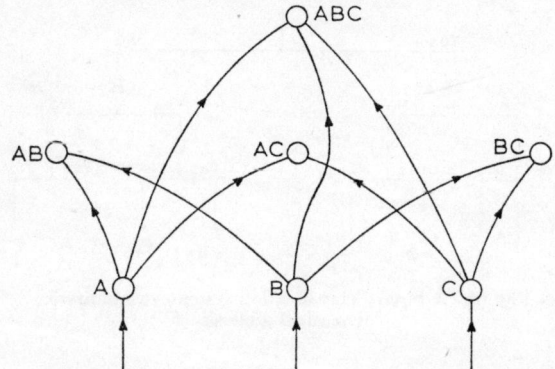

Fig. 68. A classification scheme (after Uttley)

The question arises how can we distinguish between so many different smells? The mechanism would appear to be essentially one of classification. For instance, smell A might excite a set of olfactory cells with characteristic a, smell B might likewise excite olfactory cells b, smells A and B occurring together might excite a set of olfactory cells ab sensitive to the combination, etc. Dr. Albert Uttley, of the National Physical Laboratory, Teddington, who has been responsible for a great deal of pioneering research in the field of classification, and pattern recognition, represents such a classification system as in Fig. 68. The classification system shown in the diagram is based on a binary system which means that each variable can only exist in one of two states. For example, A exists or it does not exist. If A, B and C exist simultaneously then all "cells" are excited. But if B is not present only three cells are excited, namely A, C and AC. The process can be clearly identified with classification. Many real life classification and identification systems are of a similar kind. For example, cheques and money orders are now coded in such a way that they can be automatically sorted for transmitting to the appropriate bank—the coding is of a binary character and identifies the bank to which a particular cheque is directed. The process is one of pattern recognition which leads to classification.

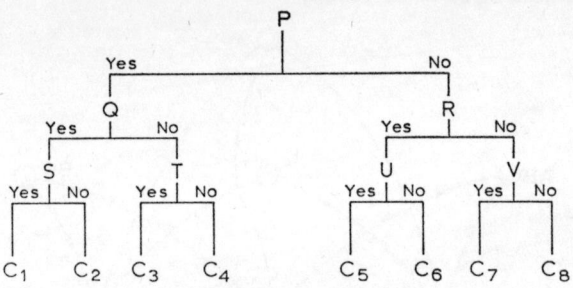

Fig. 69. A binary classification system—a qualitative chemical analysis

In another field let us consider the carrying out of a simple qualitative chemical analysis. It is a logical operation involving the processes of discrimination and pattern recognition. In some respects it is similar to the game of "20 questions". Consider a hypothetical testing sequence. Let P, Q, . . ., U, V, correspond to specific chemical tests for a group of eight chemical compounds and let the tests follow a sequence such as shown in Fig. 69. The testing sequence shown will determine which one of the eight compounds $(C_1, C_2, \ldots, C_8)$ can be identified with the sample under test. What we do in effect is to determine the pattern appropriate to a particular compound and to recognize the compound by means of the pattern itself.

THE LEARNING PROCESS

A particular test sequence may proceed as follows:

(i) If P is positive, proceed to Q;
(ii) If P is negative, proceed to R;
(iii) If Q is positive, proceed to S;
(iv) If Q is negative, proceed to T;
(v) If R is positive, proceed to U;
(vi) If R is negative, proceed to V;
(vii) If U is positive, we identify the compound C_5; if it is negative, the compound is identified as C_6, etc.

The compound identification table may be as follows:

Tests, P and Q and S positive identifies C_1.

P and Q positive and S negative identifies C_2.

P and Q and T positive identifies C_3.

P and Q positive and T negative identifies C_4.

P negative and R and U positive identifies C_5.

P and U negative and R positive identifies C_6.

P and R negative and V positive identifies C_7.

P and R and V negative identifies C_8.

The patterns we have considered may be described as "deterministic" which means that they have been established before the classification process was started. There is no uncertainty and no ambiguity. But to determine the patterns in the first place it is probable that a trial and error learning process, and hence information feedback channels, must have been involved.

The classification model shown in Fig. 68 may be given additional interesting properties if, for example, each cell incorporates a simple counting routine whereby the probability of the cell being excited, when the next stimulus is applied, can be stored. When modified in this way the classification model can be used to demonstrate pattern recognition in the case of non-deterministic, or probabilistic, systems. An important application, which we consider below, is the learning phenomenon which has been called "classical conditioning", or the conditioned reflex.

The Conditioned Reflex

The learning process covers a wide spectrum. On the one hand it may apply to the process whereby a child learns to blink his eye when a fly approaches it, while on the other it may apply to the study in depth of some newly developed mathematical techniques. In the first case we have an example of a conditioned reflex, in the second case we have an example of complex problem-solving. Both may be regarded as processes of learning.

The environment in which we live is so complex and dynamic, in the sense of changing continuously, that learning through habituation, which is another way of describing conditioned learning, will not carry us too far. In addition, we must establish cognitive powers which depend on the establishment, at the highest levels of our consciousness, of patterns of perception which are built up as the result of experience especially in problem-solving. We find therefore that the process of learning may be regarded as a hierarchy of processes taking place at higher and higher levels in the central nervous system. In this context habituation must be regarded as a low-level process which normally involves the motor system and low levels of the central nervous system.

But in order to provide a basis for understanding, or attempting to understand, the higher level learning processes we must understand the low-level learning processes. Conditioned learning is a good starting point.

At the beginning of the present century a Russian physiologist, Ivan Pavlov, who was carrying out research on the digestive process, obtained the first experimental evidence of a conditioned reflex. He discovered that if, before presenting a dog with food, a bell was rung, then, after a certain number of repetitions of this procedure the dog salivated immediately upon hearing the bell in spite of the fact that no food was present. This might appear at first sight to be a comparatively trivial observation but it nevertheless gave rise, and is still giving rise, to massive research programmes in the field of learning. It was a breakthrough in experimental psychology of the highest order. Of course, Pavlov carried out his experiments very precisely, and under controlled conditions, so that they could be repeated. He measured, for example, the amount of salivation and correlated it with the number of times the bell and the food had been paired. One immediate conclusion that he reached was that the dog learned to associate food with the ringing of a bell, and that this pattern was established so firmly in the neural network of the dog's brain that a conditioned response was evoked. Furthermore, it was an involuntary response.

Figure 70 attempts to show diagrammatically how the conditioned response arises. The occurrences of bell ringing, food present, and salivation are represented in the diagram by square

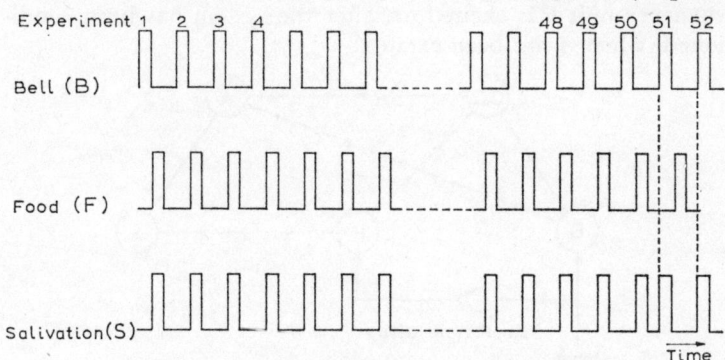

Fig. 70. Nature of conditioned learning (Pavlov's experiments)

pulses. If condition B (bell) is followed by F (food) say 50 times within a given time period, we may find in the 51st experiment that salivation is activated when the bell rings before the food arrives.

Pavlov dealt also with the question of the "extinction", or forgetting, of the conditioned response. He sought answers to such questions as how many times does the dog salivate when the bell rings in spite of the fact that food does not follow the bell ringing? Clearly, however well conditioned the dog might be at a given time, if subsequently the conditioning process is discontinued, there will come a time when ringing the bell is no longer associated in the dog's brain with the imminent arrival of food.

Consider next how the Pavlov learning experiments can be simulated by a model—a sort of mechanized "Pavlovian dog". The object is to demonstrate that the associative patterns which evolve in the dog's brain, during the experiments, can be represented approximately in terms of what we call conditional probabilities. The approach is related to the classification processes discussed earlier and, as already pointed out, is based on counting. A model of the system is shown in Fig. 71.

The units B and F correspond to bell ringing and food available respectively—the small triangle represents the fact that there is always a short delay between the bell ringing and the food arriving. The unit S corresponds to the salivation process. It is excited whenever unit F is excited or, after the system has been conditioned, when A has been excited.

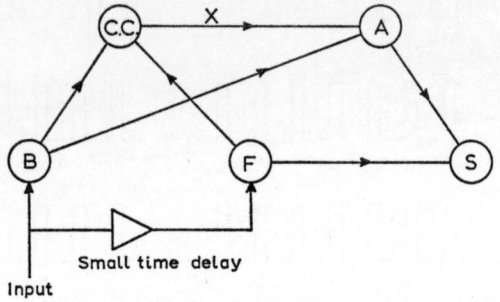

Fig. 71. Model of conditioned learning

The unit denoted by CC is a coincidence counter which is assumed to have a threshold value. During the period of the experiments this unit counts the number of coincidences of B and F and, in addition, it has a built-in divider which computes the number of coincidences divided by the number of times B alone has been excited. In mathematical language the CC unit continually determines a conditional probability, namely, the probability that F is paired with B. The conditional probability is written $p(F/B)$, which can be read as the probability of food (F) given bell (B). Now if $p(F/B)$ is greater than a fraction, say K, the threshold value, and K has the value, say, 0·8, the system is said to be in a conditioned state. When this happens we regard the unit CC as being excited, and the line X shown in Fig. 71 as being energized. The unit A is a two-input AND, or conjunction, unit, as discussed in Donald Fink's book on "Computers and the Human Mind", Chapter 6. If, and only if, the two inputs to A are energized, then the output from A is also energized. This is a basic, and very important, element in digital computers and, in a highly complicated form, in the human brain because the neuron has properties similar to a multi-input AND unit. The S unit, which in the Pavlovian experiments corresponds to the state of salivation, is excited if either the input from A is energized, in which case the system is conditioned, or the input from F is energized. The operation of the simple model can be summarized as follows:

The input conditions may be typified as one of the following two possibilities:

(a) B (the bell rings) is excited but no F (food) follows,

or,

(b) B is excited and is followed a short time interval later by F.

The output responses of the system are

(c) S is excited (the dog salivates),

or,

(d) S is not excited (the dog does not salivate).

Suppose the total number of tests carried out when either of the input conditions (a) or (b) applies is N. Suppose that of these N tests condition (b) applies Q times. If N and Q are sufficiently large numbers the conditional probability of food arriving after the bell rings is written $p(F/B)$, and in the present case this can be written approximately as Q/N. Hence, approximately, for large values of N,

$$p(F/B) = Q/N.$$

If $p(F/B)$ is greater than a constant K which may be of the order of 0·8, that is

$$p(F/B) > K,$$

the system becomes conditioned and line X, shown in Fig. 71, is energized. The coincidence-counter unit not only determines the ratio Q/N and continually updates it (in order to keep the current value of the conditional probability of F given B up to date), but it also determines whether or not this ratio is equal to or greater than K, in which case the output of the coincidence counter (CC) is energized. When the system is in a conditioned state S will be excited immediately B is excited. For example, A responds when both its inputs are energized together, but X is energized and hence A's output is energized when B is excited and S is accordingly excited.

The nature of conditioned learning has been treated in some detail because it is of great importance to an understanding of the learning process, and because of its value in the development of machines with learning capabilities, and in studies of animal and human behaviour.

The model, Fig. 71, which gives a visual picture of the nature of conditioned behaviour, is also important because it exemplifies how information flow diagrams have widespread application. Furthermore, physical models based on the conceptual or mathematical model shown in Fig. 71 have been built and have helped behavioural scientists to understand various facets of the learning process. One such model was built by Dr. Grey Walter; it is called CORA which stands for Conditioned Reflex Analogue.

A glance at Fig. 71 reveals that the conditioned learning model as it stands does not incorporate information feedback. And we might conclude that associative learning does not involve feedback. But if we penetrate more deeply, in the sense of considering the problem as a component part of a somewhat bigger problem, we arrive at a different conclusion. See, for example, Fig. 73.

It has been established that associative learning, resulting from associative linkages in the neural network of the brain, only arises when a reward is involved. Reward in this sense is to be interpreted as widely as possible to include all forms of pleasure. It may be argued therefore that information concerning the *effect* of the associative linkage is fed back to a centre in the brain where the associative linkage has been created. When the effect is identified with a desirable, in the sense of pleasure, response the information feedback tends to strengthen the associative link. On the other hand, if no reward is forthcoming as a result of the association, the information feedback causes the link, or bond, to be weakened. It is interesting to compare the role of information feedback in associative, or conditioned learning, with the role of feedback in trial and error learning. The close correspondence between the two will be apparent and we conclude that perhaps associative learning may be considered as a form of trial-and-error learning. In trial-and-error learning an association is established between the response and the reward while in conditioned learning an association is established between two stimuli. There is a significant difference.

An important example of associative learning is the "learning to read" process or alternatively learning a foreign language. In the early stages we perceive each word separately but in time we begin to associate words, and to perceive phrases or, as the behavioural scientist G. A. Miller has expressed it, we handle a "chunk" of information all at once. Learning by association implies a predictive capability and this is one reason why it helps us to read more quickly. It also explains why, although we begin to read a foreign language comparatively well, we may still have difficulty in understanding a person who speaks the foreign language because our auditory associations are not as well developed as our visual associations.

Previously we considered briefly Thorndike's experiments in which by pressing an appropriate lever a cat escaped from a cage and obtained food placed outside the cage. It has been pointed out, by some psychologists, that the process whereby the cat, in a sequence of experiments, gradually learns to press the correct lever and to open the cage, exemplifies another form of conditioned learning. In the classical experiments of Pavlov a dog learned to associate two stimuli (bell ringing and food). But in Thorndike's experiments the conditioning is carried out "backwards" so to speak. The cat begins to associate a response (for instance, the opening of the door of a cage) with an operation such as pressing a lever—the latter may be pressed by the cat's paw or its nose or its body. This class of conditioning is generally called "operant" conditioning to distinguish it from "classical" conditioning. This demonstrates another link between Pavlovian conditioning and trial-and-error learning.

Pattern Recognition

The process of classifying information, things, people, etc. giving rise to the idea of recognizing patterns was introduced earlier.

The patterns we considered were all deterministic in the sense that the pattern was built into a process. For instance, in the case of the sense of smell the olfactory receptors are pre-programmed in such a way that they are excited by particular types of molecules (which have characteristic "smells"). In the case of cheque sorting, a code identifying the bank which issued the cheque is printed on the cheque. In the case of qualitative analysis of chemical compounds the series of tests to be undertaken is laid down and so on.

But in the case of learning through a conditioning process the process is not pre-programmed. This means in effect that the human being, or the animal, actually develops patterns in the central nervous system as the experiment proceeds or as life continues. Even in the comparatively simple associative learning experiments, carried out by Pavlov, the animal learned a pattern, while in Thorndike's experiments with the cat in the cage, the cat learned a pattern of association between a lever and the availability of food. A priori, these patterns, respectively, were not available, they were developed through learning processes. Such patterns, and life is concerned with countless numbers of them, are non-deterministic, perhaps subject to changes in the environment, and certainly probabilistic in character (we referred to such situations in a previous chapter as "stochastic" processes). Usually we can regard the pattern as having been defined when we know all the relevant probabilities and conditional probabilities involved. Problem-solving, which can be regarded as a form of learning at a high level in the learning hierarchy, may involve complex patterns. The patterns may, for instance, be developed from multiple associations and experiences which have been memorized, or as a result of an extremely important attribute which we call intuition.

Many readers will, if they have not already done so, come across the term "gestalt". Gestalt is a German word which means a configuration which has characteristics more broadly based than those of its parts. A poem has a great deal more meaning and significance than the meaning of the individual words which appear in it. Likewise, the scientist may conclude that a whole pattern, or structure, has much more significance than its components. This is the reason why throughout this book I have emphasized the importance of such techniques as the representation of systems and processes by flow diagrams, or signal flowgraphs, or by models of a physical or mathematical kind. When we have established the flowgraph, or the model, we have already recognized basic patterns which may give important clues concerning system behaviour.

We will consider now the recognition and description of patterns which are probabilistic in nature. They are the basis of learning in all its forms, of discovering and of creating. They are worthy of our consideration.

As an example of how a pattern may be developed and, as a result, how the predictability of the associated system or process can be enhanced, we will consider an example which, although it has no practical significance, illustrates the general idea of pattern generation.

Suppose we have two urns, one black and the other white. For convenience we designate them urn B and urn W. In each urn there are a large number of tiny black (b) and white (w) balls—perhaps tens of thousands of them. We are required to determine the proportion of b to w balls in each urn. A perfectly satisfactory method of proceeding is to pick balls at random from, say, urn B, and to keep count of the number of b and w balls selected and subsequently returned to the urn. The random selection process continues until perhaps one or two thousand selections have been made. At this stage if x black balls and $(1000 - x)$ white balls have been selected an approximation to the required ratio is $x/(1000 - x)$.

As the selection and counting processes continue we will probably find that the ratio of the number of b balls to w balls $x/(N - x)$ approaches a constant value as N becomes larger. But it is important to stress that unless we carry on the process for a very long time, perhaps involving tens of thousands of selections, the value we obtain for the ratio is only approximate. To obtain the absolute value of the ratio we would, of course, need an infinite number of selections. A similar process will determine the ratio of b to w balls, or rather an approximation to it, in urn W.

If we record the aggregate number of b and w balls selected after 100, 200, . . ., etc. selections and express the results as percentages of b and w balls for each urn, the results may be as given in the following table.

Number of Selections	Urn B % of b	% of w	Urn W % of b	% of w
100	23	77	66	34
200	$19\frac{1}{2}$	$80\frac{1}{2}$	62	38
300	$21\frac{1}{3}$	$78\frac{2}{3}$	$60\frac{2}{3}$	$39\frac{1}{3}$
1000	20·2	79·8	60·1	39·9
2000	20·05	79·95	59·9	40·1

We might conclude that the ratio of w to b balls in urn B is approximately 4:1 and the ratio of b to w balls in urn W is approximately 3:2.

What in fact we have done is to establish probability patterns which, as the experiment continues, will give us a closer and closer approximation to the actual ratios of black to white balls in each urn. The minimum number of selections required in order to determine the b to w ratios with an expectancy of accuracy greater than, say, 99% constitutes a well-known problem in probability theory which need not concern us. Knowledge of the ratios provides us with the means of predicting, with maximum chance of success, the nature of the next selection.

Now suppose we change the experiment and incidentally make it more interesting. The object of the experiment is still to determine the probability of randomly selecting say a black ball from urn B and from urn W respectively. But we change the procedure as follows. Suppose we begin the experiment by picking a ball from urn B and suppose it is a black ball. Having returned it to the urn we pick another ball from urn B and if it is black we repeat the process. But if it is a white ball we make the next selection from urn W. In other words, the urn chosen for the next selection is determined by the selection which has just been made.

The above process is in fact an elementary example of a first-order Markov Process which may be described simply as a process in which the next state of a system depends exclusively on its present state. The study of Markov Processes is of considerable interest to some mathematicians. Further, during the past decade, Markov Processes have provided mathematical models for a large number of physical phenomena and engineering systems. And by no means least they are proving of great value in the modelling of the learning process. Although, in this book, little more than a definition of the nature of an elementary form of Markov Process is given, the idea has been introduced because of its increasing importance in science.

The "ball selecting" process, outlined above, can be described in terms of a special class of flowgraph in which each branch has allocated to it a "transition probability". In Fig. 72, for example, the branch $B \to W$ is assigned the transition probability p_{BW}.

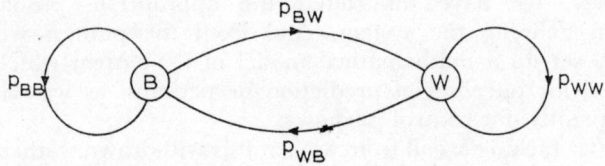

Fig. 72. A simple Markov process—transition probabilities in an urn experiment

It is the probability of picking a white ball from urn B. Similarly p_{BB} is the probability of picking a black ball from urn B, and p_{WB} and p_{WW} are the respective probabilities of picking a black and a white ball from urn W.

We can regard the transition probabilities as conditional probabilities in the sense that p_{BW} might be described as the probability of W given state B—it would be written as $p(W/B)$.

As the experiment proceeds we find that our estimates of the transitional, or conditional, probabilities change because more and more data become available. If, for example, we keep count of the withdrawals from each urn we can draw up a table of probabilities, usually called a probability matrix. The entries are continuously updated. The matrix provides a pattern based on which prediction of the next selection can be made. In the early stages of its development the value of the matrix, as a predictor, is small but as more and more experiments are carried out the true nature of the pattern begins to emerge.

The matrix is as shown below:

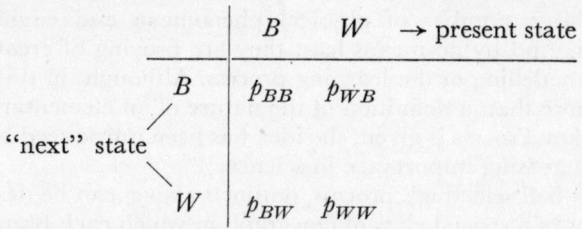

We might find, for example, that after a large number of selections $p_{BB} \to 0.82$, $p_{BW} \to 0.18$, $p_{WB} \to 0.41$, $p_{WW} \to 0.59$. At this stage we might conclude that, to the desired degree of accuracy, we have discovered the appropriate probability pattern defining the system. And from the pattern we can readily set up a mathematical model of the system which can be used for purposes of prediction or perhaps, as we will see subsequently, for control purposes.

If after picking a ball from an urn it is withdrawn, rather than returned, the transition probabilities will be much more complex and the patterns will be in a state of continuous change. Models of this kind have proved valuable in studying such phenomena as the diffusion of gases.

The value of pattern development and recognition in the learning process will be evident. Indeed it would perhaps be correct to state that the development of patterns, in the sense of discovering structure in knowledge, is a prerequisite to all learning. And the acquisition of knowledge requires experimentation in the sense of "probing the environment". In the planning of an experiment we first state an hypothesis which we hope to prove or to disprove. We then conduct a series of experiments in which perhaps a system, or process, is stimulated by an "input", and the result of the stimulation is recorded as a "response". Pattern development and recognition calls for an association, often probabilistic, between the various inputs and the corresponding responses. The pattern so obtained is examined in the light of the hypothesis, and, as a result of the examination, the experimenter devises modified inputs and the process is repeated until the pattern is developed adequately to prove or to disprove the hypothesis. By its nature the system is essentially an information feedback system.

THE LEARNING PROCESS

In some respects we may regard the patterns developed in our brains as "models" of the environment or of a particular task. Carrying out a task, unless we have performed it many times before, calls for learning. If the task is simple, the corresponding pattern or model will be established quickly. But if the task is complex and it is necessary to develop many associative patterns the learning process may be lengthy. In Fig. 73 I have attempted to show diagrammatically how the associative patterns are established in the performance of a given task. The "control"

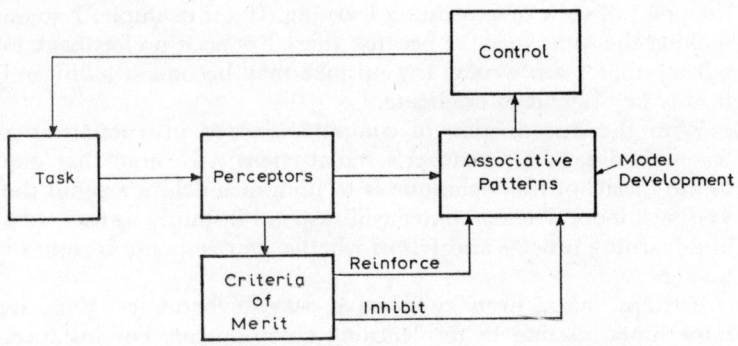

Fig. 73. Development of associative patterns (models) in learning a task

element in the system will normally consist of human muscles and their extensions in the form of tools and instruments which are required to perform the task. The pattern, or model, will be developed through both subconscious and conscious brain activity. One thing is clear, it is that without feedback we would neither establish the required patterns nor perform the task.

Expediting Learning

In this chapter, I hope the impression has not been given that learning is a branch of feedback control theory or cybernetics. On the other hand, if I have shown that some of the ideas stimulated by cybernetic science have thrown some light on the learning process I shall be happy. Let us pursue the topic a little further.

In a world of rapid technological change ideas concerning how the learning processes can be expedited are welcome. If we think of the learning process as a feedback process we come to the conclusion that delays around the information loops may not be conducive to speedy learning. Such delays may occur between our taking a particular step, or decision, or action, and the result of the action which either reinforces, or inhibits, the associative patterns which gave rise to the action in the first place. In other words, the sooner we know how well, or badly, we have performed a task, perhaps a quiz, the better it is from the point of view of expediting learning. If, for example, I go on making the same mistake because there has been no feedback to tell me that I am wrong, my mistake may become a habit and it may be difficult to eradicate.

With the introduction of computer-assisted instruction as a teacher's aid (not a teacher's replacement), we note that one of the merits of the technique is to minimize delays around the feedback loop. The computer will respond instantly at each step in a learning process and tell us whether our response is right or wrong.

Perhaps, also, in a qualitative way, cybernetics gives us some hints relating to the learning environment. For instance, if the environment is static, as in the majority of repetitive tasks, the associated patterns established in the brain are static and the degree of feedback necessitated is minimal. But minimal feedback in the learning process implies a low level of consciousness because changes are not anticipated. We become habituated. If, in these circumstances, changes do in fact occur low-level consciousness may result in our inability to recognize change. In such conditions man becomes a programmed system which may be characterized by an inability to learn and hence to adapt. This is fortunately an extreme condition.

On the other hand, if the environment is dynamic and exciting the pattern development and recognition processes must also, for successful adaptation, be dynamic. Multiple feedback channels continually pour information into the brain to expedite pattern building and intuitive thought. Unlike the algorithmic (programmed) nature of conditioned learning, the learning process, which involves discovery and intuition, is of a heuristic kind and hence is not susceptible to programmed treatment. Above all

THE LEARNING PROCESS

consciousness is stimulated and the recognition of almost imperceptible changes in patterns is expedited and utilized. The trend must therefore be toward learning environments which excite the curiosity. This is one of the great merits of the scientific laboratory as a learning environment.

There is another potentially exciting application of cybernetic principles to learning. I refer to the new advances in computer technology which have been described as machine-aided cognition. Techniques such as "sketchpad", whereby a scientist or engineer can communicate directly with a computer by means of a special cathode ray tube and a "light" pencil, are already well advanced. In such systems the research worker states his problem in specially coded form on the cathode ray tube, in much the same way as he would state the problem using paper and pencil, and the computer carries out the computations required, usually in fractions of a second, and flashes back the result in a form which is readily interpreted. In this way a sort of man-machine dialogue is established and this means that the capabilities of man on the one hand and machine on the other are being used to the full capacity—the human as an intuitive and inductive thinker, the machine as an ultra high-speed data processor and computer. For the first time in history man's ideas will be tried out, usually through the modelling process, with incredible speed. And there is reason to believe that man's creative powers in all fields of human endeavour will be enhanced. The usefulness of man-computer systems in facilitating learning is likely to be spectacular.

In spite of the probability of the widespread introduction of a variety of teaching aids, especially the use of computers in the teaching process, and the thrilling prospect of machine-aided cognition, the teacher's role, far from being diminished in importance, will probably be enhanced. The teacher can recognize behavioural patterns in students through many feedback channels which, by their nature, are not measurable and hence cannot be utilized by a machine. Moreover, it is often the almost imperceptible changes in response which the good teacher can use to improve his approach to a subject. In addition the teacher can expedite the learning process by sub-dividing tasks into their basic components. He can demonstrate skills and stimulate the student into undertaking experiments on his own. He can provide success criteria perhaps on an individual rather than a class basis. But above all the teacher who is enthusiastic about his subject, and understanding of his role as teacher and friend, can induce high morale and confidence in the student.

The teaching and learning processes interact in a multiplicity of ways exemplifying the feedback principle in its most profound milieu.

Some Suggestions for Further Reading

WIENER, N., *Cybernetics*, John Wiley & Sons, New York.
SUTTON, O. G., *Mathematics in Action*, Harper Bros., New York.
BAYLISS, L. E., *Living Control Systems*, New Science Series, English Universities Press.
KILMISTER, C. W., *Language, Logic and Mathematics*, New Science Series, English Universities Press.
PORTER, A., *Servomechanisms*, Methuen Physical Monographs.
HOLLINGDALE, S. H., and TOOTILL, G. C., *Electronic Computers*, Pelican Book A524.
TUSTIN, A., *The Mechanism of Economic Systems*, Harvard University Press.
FINK, D., *Computers and the Human Mind*, Doubleday and Co.

Index

Index

Accelerometer, 3, 43
Accuracy, dynamic, 36, 67
　static, 36, 67
Adaptation to environment, 20
Adaptive process, 128
Aircraft control, 56, 74
Algebraic equations solution by
　　flowgraph, 103
Algorithmic, 148
Alternating current, 50
　reference voltage, 50
Ambient conditions, 63
Amplitude modulation, 52
Analogue computers, 78
Anti-aircraft defence, 29
　fire control, 50
Aristotle, 126
Associative learning, 126
Astronaut, 2
Astronomy, 20
Automata, 79
Automatic regulator, 55
Automation, 21
Autonomic nervous system, 14

Bang-bang control, 62–66
Bellman, R., 4
Binary digital code, 52
　signals, 53
　word, 53
Biological evolution, 19
Blackett, P. M. S., 29
Block diagram, 5, 37, 89
Bohr, N., 80

Cannon, W. B., 26
Carrier signal, 52
Cathode ray tube, 120
Cerebellar attaxia, 124
Chemical plant, 78
　analysis, 134
Cheque sorting, 142
Classification of data, 133
Closed loop, 60
Coded data, 35
Coding techniques, 52
Communication, 27, 35
Comparator, 6
Computer (vii), 72
　Analogue, 90
　Assisted instruction, 148
　Control, 30
　Digital, 5, 29, 90
　Flow diagram, 112
　Hybrid, 90
　On-line, 15, 30
　Program, 5
　Programming, 94, 111–112
　Simulation, 9
Conditional probabilities, 138
Conditioned reflex, 136
Control (viii)
　automatic, 2
　biological, 14
　engineering, 2, 3
　hierarchy of, 16
　optimal, 17
　regulatory, 17
　rod, 11

155

INDEX

Cramer's Rub, 105
Critical damping, 48
Critical path, (v)
Cybernetics (vii), 55
  Biological example, 12, 14
  Definition of, 2
  Economic example, 14

Dampers, 48
Data transmission, 49
Decisions, 3, 5
Delay-line storage and system, 113
Derivative of error, 120
Differential calculus, 47
Differential equation, 47
Digitalizing, 52
DNA, 81
Drebbel, C., 23
Drucker Peter, (v)
Dynamic behaviour, 39, 42
  equilibrium, 47

Econometrics, 28
Economic control system, 15
  system, 4
Electro-cardiograms, 52
Electro-magnetic relay, 64
Electronic amplifier, 12, 25
Energy conversion, 35, 36
Environment, 2, 71
Equilibrium, physiological, 26
  state, 13
Error-actuated system, 8, 10, 17
Error signal, 8, 35, 60
Exponential delay, 41
  response, 39
  time-constant, 40, 43, 74

Feedback (vii), 1, 55
  amplifier, 25, 55
  channels, 74
  loop, 6
  signal, 41
Fink, D., 138
Flowgraph, 93, 143
Forced oscillations, 116
Frequency modulation, 52
Frequency response studies, 117

Gain of servo, 68–71, 108, 113
Gestalt, 142
Goal-seeking, 19
Graph theory, 93
Gravitational field, 2
Gravity, 2
Gyroscope, 3

Harmonic motion, 48
Heisenberg Uncertainty Principle, 37
Heuristic, 148
Hipparchus, 20
Homeostasis (vii), 13, 26, 100
Hooke's Law, 44
Human brain, 33
  operator, 50, 56, 57, 71–77
  reaction time, 33, 57, 75, 77
Human factors engineering, 28, 29, 71, 78
Hunting response, 113
Hydraulic control, 74
  model, 97–98

Industrial Revolution, 22
Inertia force, 45
Inertial guidance, 3

Information feedback, 1–5
  biological, 12
  in model, 83
  negative, 5, 8
  neural, 13
  position, 5, 8
Information flow diagram, 93
Inherent stability, 110
Input shaft, 60
Instrument delay, 39
Instrumentation, 35
Integral of error, 67, 98
Interdependence of variables, 93
Iterative process, 111

Joystick, 74

Kelvin, Lord, 34
  dictum, 34
Kepler's Law, 15
Keynes, Lord, 102

Law of exponential decay, 39, 42, 87
Learning, (ix)
Linear system, 94
Load, 60
  disturbance, 61
Looprule, 105

Machine tools, numerical control, 31
Magnetic tape, 32
Man the creator, 22
Management science, 30
Man-machine systems, 29, 78
  languages, 72
Manual control, 25, 57, 72

Manufacturing process, 4
Markov Process, 144–146
Mason, S. J., 93
Matrix, 88
  algebra, 89
  model, 89
Maxwell, Clerk, 24, 80
McLuhan, Marshall, (v)
Measurement, 34, 35
Mesthene, E. G., (v)
Miller, G. A., 141
Models (viii), 79–106
  as hypothesis, 80
  mathematical, 80–93
  physical, 90
Multi-loop control system, 75

Natural frequency, 92, 116
Naval gunnery, 25
Navigation, 2, 20
Neuron, 3, 20
Neutron flux density, 11
Newton's Laws of Motion, 43, 47, 86
Noise, 53, 118
Noisy channel, 52
Non-linear damping, 91
Non-Newtonian fluid, 92
Nuclear fission, 10
Nuclear power station, 10
Nuclear reactor, 10, 17, 78
Nyquist, H., 25
Nyquist stability criterion, 113

Olfactory cells, 133
On-line process controllers, 105
On-off control, 62, 64
Open-loop control, 6
Operations research, 28
Oscillatory behaviour, 26, 41

Output shaft, 60
Overshoot, 77

Paleolithic man, 21
Pappin, D., 23
Patterns, (ix), 136, 146
   recognition, 19, 134, 141
Pavlov, Ivan, 136
Pilot, 74
Position control system, *see* Servomechanism
Potentiometer, 49
Prediction, 20
Protection systems, 17
Protective device, 10
Pupil of eye, 14

Radar, 2, 27, 29, 78
Radio link, 49
Radioactive decay, 87
Recognition of change, 33
Redundancy, 52
Regulation, 10
Regulatory system, 17
Remote monitoring, 52
Retina, 14

Sampled data signal, 52
Samuel, Arthur, 127, 132
Self-regulating system, 100
Self-stabilizing, 124
Sensors, 3, 13, 33, 37, 72
Servo, *see* servomechanism
Servomechanism, (vii), 24, 55, 77
   elements of, 58–60
Ship's rudder control, 55
Signal flowgraphs, 93–104
Simulator, 29, 84
Sketchpad, 149

Slide rule, 90
Snow, C. P., (v)
Space satellite, 15, 27, 78
Speed of response, 58, 69
Spending levels, 15
Spring force, 45
Stability, (ix), 107–125
   definition of, 108
   Nyquist criterion of, 25
Steady-state, 39, 41, 44
Step function, 39, 45, 75, 76
Stochastic process, 5, 132, 142
Stretch receptor, 13, 74
Sutton, O. G., 80
Synaptic junction, 13
Synchro system, 50, 51, 58
SYNCOM III, 16
Systemic arts, 28
Systems engineering, 28

Telescopes, optical and radio, 28, 61
Television, 15
Temperature control, 6
Thermal expansion, 85
Thermocouple, 36
Thermometer, 36
Thermostatic control system, 6, 62
Thorndike, E. L., 129, 130
Time constant, 40, 43, 99
Time-delay, 36, 64, 74, 75
   finite, 38, 39, 77
Time integral of error, 68
Torque, 55
Tracking error, 69
Traffic control, 30, 31
Trajectory of shell, 86
Transient behaviour, 45
   state, 45

INDEX

Transition probability, 145
Travelling salesman problem, 88
Trial and error learning, 129
Tustin, A., 29, 93

Unstable behaviour in biological systems, 107
Urrley, A. M., 133

Variable, control, 34, 35, 74
object, 34

Velocity control, 56
Velocity lag, 69, 119
 compensation, 71
Viscous friction force, 45
 coefficient, 46, 48, 91, 119
Voltmeter, 41

Walter Grey, 132, 140
Watt, James, 22
Wiener, Norbert, 2, 29, 56, 124
Williams, F. C., 27
World War II developments, 77